southwest Alaska

Yunnan Province, China

western Bolivia

southwestern Australia

La Amistad International Park, Costa Rica

Gondwana Link, Australia

design for
a living world

Yucatán Peninsula, Mexico

design for
a living world

EDITORS
Ellen Lupton and Abbott Miller

ESSAY BY
Andy Grundberg

PRINCIPAL PHOTOGRAPHY
Ami Vitale

CONTRIBUTORS
Gabrielle Antoniadis, Sara Elliott, and Emily Whitted

Design inspired by The Nature Conservancy's
Campaign for a Sustainable Planet

The Nature Conservancy
Protecting nature. Preserving life.™

Smithsonian
Cooper-Hewitt, National Design Museum

www.nature.org/design

Yunnan Province, China

contents

foreword   16
PAUL WARWICK THOMPSON

preface   18
MARK TERCEK

truth and material   22
ELLEN LUPTON AND ABBOTT MILLER

pictures, places, people, things   30
ANDY GRUNDBERG

36   federated states of micronesia
VEGETABLE IVORY AND BLACK PEARL,
TED MUEHLING

52   australia
RASPBERRY JAM WOOD, STEPHEN BURKS

68   costa rica
COCOA, YVES BÉHAR

84   bolivia
FSC-CERTIFIED PLYWOOD, ABBOTT MILLER

100   bolivia
FSC-CERTIFIED HARDWOOD AND JIPIJAPA,
KATE SPADE NEW YORK

116   alaska
SALMON LEATHER, ISAAC MIZRAHI

132   mexico
CHICLE, HELLA JONGERIUS

148   idaho
ORGANIC WOOL, CHRISTIEN MEINDERTSMA

164   china
BAMBOO, EZRI TARAZI

180   maine
FSC-CERTIFIED RED MAPLE, MAYA LIN

contributors   197
acknowledgments   198
credits   200

foreword

A Palau spear fisherman hunts for fish outside Pohnpei's reef in the Federated States of Micronesia. The bounty of Pohnpei's sea and forests has sustained people for centuries.

In 1984, Cooper-Hewitt, National Design Museum presented an exhibition entitled *The Golden Eye*. The popular exhibition blended traditional South Asian craftsmanship with Western design thinking. Twenty-five years later, Cooper-Hewitt is proud to bring you *Design for a Living World*—a project conceived and developed by The Nature Conservancy—which again brings together two seemingly disparate worlds: international product design and the natural environment.

As with *The Golden Eye*, our mission with *Design for a Living World* is to encourage cross-fertilization. This exhibition is timely: With the new U.S. administration committed to creating green-collar jobs and investing in clean, renewable technologies, Cooper-Hewitt and The Nature Conservancy are combining to demonstrate how we, as designers and consumers, must rethink our choice of materials and our relationship with the land. *Design for a Living World* points us in a "new" direction by challenging a talented group of designers to make beautiful contemporary designs inspired by nature and considerate of its resources.

I extend sincere congratulations and thanks to Mark Tercek, President and CEO of The Nature Conservancy, and all of his colleagues for organizing this very vital exhibition in collaboration with Cooper-Hewitt. I also applaud the design duo of Abbott Miller of Pentagram and Ellen Lupton, Cooper-Hewitt's Curator of Contemporary Design, who teamed to design this extraordinary exhibition and accompanying catalogue.

The exhibition presentation at Cooper-Hewitt is made possible in part by Enid and Lester Morse. Additional support is provided by Esme Usdan. The catalogue is made possible in part by the Andrew W. Mellon Foundation.

At Cooper-Hewitt, I thank Cara McCarty, Curatorial Director, for her expert guidance of the exhibition's execution, as well as Cynthia Trope, Associate Curator in the Product Design and Decorative Arts department; Cynthia Smith, contract coordinator; Jocelyn Groom, Head of Exhibitions; and Chul R. Kim, Director of Publications.

Paul Warwick Thompson, Director
Cooper-Hewitt, National Design Museum

preface

Chicle latex, used in the manufacture of chewing gum, flows from the *Manilkara zapota*, a tree that grows in the Yucatán rainforest. Here, the local *chicleros* harvest the material by cutting a network of slashes through the tree's bark. The liquid chicle flows down through these channels for collection.

Our species has always had a complicated relationship with the natural world. Nature provides the sustenance we need to survive, but it has the power to destroy us. Thus, we love it and hate it, praise it and damn it, welcome it and rebuff it. We fight hard to tame nature, but romanticize its wildness. Sometimes we love nature to its detriment and condemn its patterns unjustly.

Lately, our relationship with nature has taken center stage. Melting ice caps, rising seas, and the growing intensity of hurricanes have led people from skepticism to acceptance of human-induced climate change. Suddenly, global warming is not a distant prospect; it is an urgent concern for the health and welfare of every creature living on Earth. At the same time, our forests are disappearing to make room for agriculture and development, our lakes and oceans are becoming toxic dumping grounds, our air hangs heavy with pollutants, and countless species vanish from our planet forever.

Today, we find that we stand at the threshold of a depleted world.

We have so reshaped our planet that our very life-support system is in jeopardy. But there is still time to reverse the trend if we truly begin to envision a sustainable planet. For nearly sixty years, The Nature Conservancy has been dedicated to protecting the lands and waters that the diversity of life on Earth needs to survive. We recognize that in order for solutions to be environmentally sustainable, they must also be economically and culturally sustainable.

At its heart, sustainability is a quest for equilibrium, a balance between human use and natural regeneration. It sounds simple, but it is a principle gravely challenged by some of the most pervasive trends of our time. We are increasingly an urban society, more removed from nature than ever before. Although every product we use has its origins in nature, our physical distance from the natural world breaks the link between that product and its source. More and more, our food comes from a supermarket, not a grassland farm or ranch; and our furniture comes from a national retail chain, not a tropical hardwood forest. Nature, the foundation of human sustenance, no longer surrounds us, and we are challenged to value that which we no longer experience on a daily basis.

Though it is obscured, our connection to the natural world remains. *Design for a Living World* traces those connections by dispatching designers to specific places around the world to create functional objects that reflect and celebrate the natural landscape. Out in the field, the designers learned about a raw material's source and the communities that produce and depend upon that material for income. Each designer's final object draws inspiration from the landscape, the people, and the material in its most basic, unpolished state. Through these works of design, we are asked to consider our effect and the impact of our consumption not only on the environment, but also on the lives of those who depend on the land for their very survival.

All of the commissions undertaken for *Design for a Living World* reveal truths about the challenge and the potential of sustainable sourcing. One of the most promising areas of sustainable resource management is the work that conservation organizations are doing in partnership with communities and timber companies, promoting "good wood" from responsibly managed forests. We lose millions of acres of native forest annually to deforestation, which contributes as much as 20 percent of the greenhouse gases released into the atmosphere each year. Some of the most desirable hardwoods—like mahogany—come from tropical forests that are being rapidly depleted, often by illegal logging. Local residents lose out, since illegal logging is mostly undertaken by outsiders. Communities want to keep their forests healthy, if sustainably used, to continue to avail themselves of the income and services the forest provides.

Several designers chose to celebrate the success of community forestry projects in their work. Paulina Reyes for kate spade new york traveled to Bolivia's forests to work with local artisans to design a series of handbags made of sustainably harvested wood that had been certified by the Forest Stewardship Council (FSC). The artisans carved the wood in the centuries-old tradition of the mission-style churches in their village, connecting the final piece to both the sustainable management of a globally significant natural resource as well as to the traditions and pride of the people.

Other designers took naturally plentiful materials and creatively revealed their glamour and, likewise, a potential source of sustainable livelihood. Ted Muehling traveled to the Micronesian island of Pohnpei, in the southwestern Pacific Ocean, to source affordable and abundant black pearls and vegetable ivory seeds. The jewelry he produced from these contrasting elements of black and white transcends their humble origins. Similarly, fashion designer Isaac Mizrahi turned salmon skin—typically a waste product of the Alaskan salmon industry—into an elegant leather dress that references the fish scales from which it was made.

And other projects, including Abbott Miller's design for flat-pack plywood furniture, demonstrate the possibility of responsible and sustainable sourcing at a commercial scale. That, of course, is the consuming challenge of sustainable product design—how to affect all points in the product life cycle at a scale large enough to have a real impact without overwhelming the natural resource on which it depends.

The Nature Conservancy developed *Design for a Living World* to remind us all of our connection to the natural world and to raise awareness about the impact and promise of sustainable sourcing. Designers hold a crucial position in the supply chain, from resource to the consumer, from concept to store shelf. By fusing form and function, beauty and utility, design has the power to capture our imagination, make us love an inanimate object and want to understand it, protect it, and save it for our children. We must do the same for our shared natural heritage.

At The Nature Conservancy, we hold in our sights a vision of a sustainable planet—one where we can harness nature's fury but free its benevolent patterns; where we can thrive in cities while maintaining wilderness and our connections to it. It is a vision that reconciles the duality of our relationship to the natural world. This exhibition is one entry point to examine our own diverse roles in creating a sustainable world.

For the human race to thrive, we must choose to preserve and respect the natural world upon which we all depend. We can voraciously consume our way through our planet's resources, or we can explore new and innovative ways to use them while preventing them from being used up. We can strike a balance between consumption and conservation. It is our choice. It will be our legacy.

Mark Tercek, President and CEO
The Nature Conservancy

truth and materials

ELLEN LUPTON AND ABBOTT MILLER

Ted Muehling works with carvers in the town of Kapinga, on the island of Pohnpei, in the Federated States of Micronesia. Descendants of the Kapingamarangi people, who were forced to migrate here after a severe drought on their own island in 1916, are caught between a modern money economy they cannot afford and a life of subsistence that their land does not support. Many people in the village have turned to the handicraft trade for their livelihood.

The artifacts that furnish our dwellings and workplaces—chairs, lamps, laptops—consist of materials that have been sliced, bent, molded, and hewn into useful things. Many of the substances we think of as "natural," such as wood, bamboo, and leather, originate in living organisms, while others are mined from the earth. All of these materials, whether living or nonliving, are extracted from physical landscapes.

"Truth to materials" has been a theme in the discourse of modern design for more than a century. This principle, which celebrates the innate textures and behaviors of materials over faux finishes and applied ornament, has guided generations of designers. Today, the idea of holding true to materials is expanding in significance. As designers and consumers explore the environmental ethics of manufactured things, they seek transparency about where goods come from and how they are made.

The moment a tree is felled, it has begun a long journey of transformation from living organism to processed commodity. While many communities have made great progress toward responsibly managing their forests, illegally harvested lumber—smuggled across international borders and converted into goods for global distribution—still constitutes a sprawling black market, with fingers reaching into nearly every corner of the world economy. To help designers and consumers choose wood and other forest products that have been sourced responsibly, the Forest Stewardship Council developed a product-certification system, now considered the gold standard for forest-product certification. FSC certification—along with other third-party systems that measure the social and environmental impact of goods, such as LEED criteria for buildings, Cradle to Cradle standards for industrial products, and Fair Trade certification for agricultural goods—makes it easier for designers to obtain materials in a rigorous fashion and for consumers to make responsible choices.

Conservation principles, practices, choices: They come to light in *Design for a Living World*. To bring about the exhibition, The Nature Conservancy commissioned ten prominent designers

Designer Hella Jongerius experiments with gummy chicle—with some help from children in the *ejido*, a self-governing land cooperative unique to Mexico, *Veinte de Noviembre*. The Nature Conservancy and partner organizations are working with communities that border the forest to develop an integrated agricultural system that allows the farmers to abandon destructive slash-and-burn techniques while at the same increasing their livelihood.

to develop new uses for sustainably grown and harvested natural substances, beginning with the materials' point of origin. Each location, from the arid bush land of Australia's Gondwana Link to the lush tropical forests of Bolivia, Costa Rica, and Mexico, supports a distinctive ecosystem and provides crucial livelihoods to local communities. Each place is threatened by destructive forces, such as climate change, deforestation, and overdevelopment. In this exhibition, each place also becomes a source of design inspiration, offering a vibrant context that informs the concept, shape, and meaning of an object. *Design for a Living World* seeks to illuminate the complexity and vitality of materials at their source.

In Maya Lin's piece, the individual shape of a tree dictates the form of a bench; a gentle undulating landscape occurs after the bark is peeled and the boards are randomly placed side by side. Designers like Lin are beginning to see natural materials as a new kind of "high tech" resulting from complex (natural) systems and producing rich forms linked to the infinite variety of living things. Handbags designed by Paulina Reyes for kate spade new york feature handles and ornamental tiles made from FSC-certified *morado*, or Bolivian rosewood. The exhibition itself, designed by Abbott Miller and his team at Pentagram, is built from FSC-certified hardwood.

Design for a Living World explores less familiar substances as well, including chicle latex, salmon leather, and vegetable ivory. Chicle latex, which is found in the rainforests of Belize, Guatemala, Mexico, and Nicaragua, has no known uses apart from making chewing gum. The Nature Conservancy thus sought to explore its properties with Dutch designer Hella Jongerius, who is renowned for her laboratory-style experiments with materials. Jongerius created a series of vessels and other objects that investigate chicle latex's adhesive properties and molding characteristics. This commission offers an opportunity to look at the forest and its products from a new direction; it also aims to raise awareness of organic chewing gum, which is manufactured today by companies such as Glee Gum in Providence, Rhode Island.

Salmon leather is an unusual material with substantial industrial potential. In Alaska, commercial fisheries are the state's largest employer, and salmon drives the economy in many parts of the region. Skin discarded by canning and smoking plants can be finished into refined and durable pelts of leather using a process that is less toxic than the traditional tanning of skin from land

animals. Whereas many forms of leather manufacturing exploit creatures solely for their skins, salmon leather uses a waste product from the food industry. The Nature Conservancy commissioned prominent fashion designer Isaac Mizrahi to create garments that reveal the elegance and promise of salmon leather and aim to inspire other designers and manufacturers to do the same.

Dutch designer and textile artist Christien Meindertsma is known for projects that honor the origins of commonly used materials. For the exhibition, she used wool from sheep at Lava Lake Ranch in Idaho to create a rug made out of modular tiles that hook together. Each tile is made from 3 1/2 pounds of wool, the yield from shearing a single sheep.

On the Micronesian island of Pohnpei, the Kapingamarangi people have begun carving seeds from the ivory nut palm tree (*Metroxylon amicarum*) as an alternative to carving wood from mangrove trees, which are threatened by overharvesting. The tree's nuts, which drop naturally to the ground, have a creamy ring-shaped core with a hard, ungrained flesh—known as vegetable ivory—that is suitable for carving into small decorative objects. The Nature Conservancy commissioned the legendary jewelry designer Ted Muehling to travel to Pohnpei and develop designs using this distinctive sustainable material.

Cocoa is another forest product explored in *Design for a Living World*. Product designer Yves Béhar traveled to Costa Rica to learn how the tree is cultivated, and how the cocoa bean is harvested and processed. Rather than create a new cocoa-based food product, he crafted an elegant tool for preparing a traditional chocolate beverage consumed in La Amistad International Park, Costa Rica. The beverage is made by shaving bits of cocoa off of a hand-shaped patty. Béhar believes that in addition to enhancing the experience of making the beverage, the product may have commercial potential.

For his commission, industrial designer Stephen Burks also created a tool. After visiting Australia's vast Gondwana Link landscape, Burks conceived a device for grinding native plant materials that can then be processed into medicinal and cosmetic preparations.

Bamboo, a fast-growing grass native to China, is used in countless ways by humans, including as a building material and a food source. While industrially processed bamboo is hugely popular as a surface material, Israeli designer Ezri Tarazi chose to use it structurally. He exploited the strength, girth, and hollow

Paulina Reyes, a
designer for kate spade
new york, learns to
weave in the traditional
indigenous style in
the remote village of
Salvatierra, Bolivia,
where women have
formed a cooperative for
producing and selling
their artisanal textiles.
Here, Reyes shows the
women photos she took
of them.

core of bamboo to create a series of home furnishings that
resemble an indoor forest growing from the floor.

For the past twenty years, the expression "new materials" has
been a buzzword in the design community, often referring to
high-performance synthetics or "smart" surfaces capable of
emitting light or shifting shape or color. The commissions in
Design for a Living World explore the idea that the newest materials
of all can be familiar or overlooked substances that are ripe for
rediscovery. While the design process normally begins with
envisioning the end results—how a product will be used and, from
a conservation standpoint, how it can be recycled or reclaimed—
this exhibition reverses the process by making the point of origin
the point of inspiration.

All over the world, human populations depend on the local
landscape for their economic well-being. Increasingly, they seek
to participate in the global economy by exporting some of their
resources. Yet once the landscape is depleted, it can sustain
neither human prosperity nor diverse ecosystems. This exhibition
shows how designers can support conservation by sourcing
sustainably harvested wood and other products. They can also
promote these values to the public through effective labeling
and information systems.

Each of the commissions in *Design for a Living World* strives to
provoke conversation and to raise awareness of the origin of natural
materials. As one-of-a-kind prototypes, they reflect a continuous
thought process rather than recipes for mass production. These
designers were selected for their experimental outlook and for their
active engagement with issues of sustainability and social justice.
The heart of this exhibition lies, however, in the vital and fragile
locales from which these materials come. It is through the stories
of these places—and the people, plants, and animals living there—
that we better appreciate nature's delicate balance.

pictures, places, people, things

ANDY GRUNDBERG

Ranch managers Cheryl
and Tim Bennett, along
with their two children,
Brodie and Payson, live
at Lava Lake where they
oversee a sustainable
sheep ranching
operation.

Photography played a starring role in the 2001 exhibition *In Response to Place: Photographs from The Nature Conservancy's Last Great Places*, a commission project that in many respects provided a model for this undertaking. Here again the focus is on ways in which innovative thinking can create useful sympathies and synergies between the natural world and human culture, but the medium is design and the creator/artists on center stage are designers, not photographers. Still, in *Design for a Living World* we find photographs to be an essential component of the story.

Since its earliest days in the nineteenth century, photography has been used to connect viewers to people and places far away and in most cases remote from the viewers' experience. Explorers and scientists hired professional photographers to accompany them or learned to make photographs themselves, delighting in images that seemed to mimic reality itself and thus could be taken as indisputable evidence or fact. The sublime grandeur of the Grand Canyon and the faces and garments of Bedouins in Palestine were first brought home to awed American and European audiences by the camera. Before frequent-flier miles, most people saw the world as a procession of photographs, from stereo cards to postcards.

It was only in the twentieth century, after countless issues of *National Geographic* magazine and myriad documentations of tribal peoples by the likes of Edward S. Curtis, that we came to understand that, however truthful photographic images may seem, they remain objective only up to the point that we begin to interpret them. At that point, cultural and historical biases creep in, starting with the intentions of the person taking the picture and extending to the preconceptions that inform our own worldviews. But there is an unseen advantage to this subjectivity: photographs are useful not only because of what they tell us about their subjects, but also because of what they tell us about ourselves.

At the same time that photography has been used to describe the range and richness of the natural world and of human nature, it has been enlisted to whet our appetites for products ranging from sliced bread to new automobiles. A brand of image-making called commercial photography developed alongside modern product design, modern advertising, and modern consumer magazines to promote the pleasures of ownership and consumption. Sometimes this was largely benign, if the topic was pre-cooked spaghetti sauce, and sometimes it was to the detriment of the natural resources (e.g., oil) needed to sustain the very consumer culture the images promoted.

In short, photography has been enlisted in two simultaneous but very different projects in modern life, each of them enormously useful but also problematic in some respects: the documentation of experience outside our own, and the creation of an iconography of consumer desire. In purporting to document others, the camera often reveals or produces cultural stereotypes. It also may frame the landscape so that the ravages of human uses of the land, such as mining, are invisible and thus out of mind. Conversely, in feeding consumer appetites it can promote unthinking and unsustainable consumption of resources. Neither result is likely to help heal the planet nor to bring together the variously "developed" and "undeveloped" worlds to ensure the future of all the species, including ours.

What makes *Design for a Living World* fascinating in part is the way in which a medium distinguished by these seemingly dis-jointed practices has been brought to bear on an effort to develop sustainable habits of consumption. These images benefit the people and places that provide the raw materials used to produce finished goods, and consequently benefit the long-term preservation of precious natural habitats and biodiversity—which is to say, all of us. True, the designed objects are themselves the best testament to the ambitions of *Design for a Living World*, but unless we are standing in front of them we know them only through photo-graphs. And we know more about the places from whence their raw materials came, and the people who nurture these materials in sus-tainable ways, because we have pictures of these places and people.

Photographer Ami Vitale's work for the project is a case study in how photographs can explicate the "back story" of the productive process, from raw materials to processing, design, assembly, production, packaging, shipping, sales, and marketing. A single, perfectly lit camera image of the final product in splendid isolation may speak volumes about how our desires shape our vision, but the pleasures of reportage (or what is loosely called documentary photography) can be more complex and interesting and ultimately more satisfying. In this sense, Vitale's photographs are not so much a supplement to the project but integral to its mission.

For the past fifteen years, Vitale has worked as a photojournalist, taking pictures primarily for leading magazines and newspapers in the United States and England. She has been drawn to the developing world and to the issues of poverty, ethnic conflict, and environmental and economic exploitation that are found there all too often. For this assignment her brief was more positive: to focus on the land and inhabitants of the places selected for the designers' commissions, to show people already living in sustainable balance with the natural world around them or attempting to do so, and to illustrate the sustainable materials selected for the design projects. Her pictures also illustrate the gathering, harvesting, processing, and other steps taken in the production of these materials, from the shearing of sheep to the cooking of chicle.

As a result, these pictures in series produce something quite different than the garden-variety landscape photograph of a beautiful, distant place, the quasi-anthropological portrait of a strange and supposed primitive people, or even the elegant shot of a finished, well-designed object. Functioning narratively, they tell the story of how these things are connected in an essential chain that includes human beings as well as the natural world. They acknowledge consumption as a natural function, suggesting that we and nature are all linked together in a complex and indivisible system that has an indescribable, fragile beauty all its own.

Whether the raw material is wood or wool, bamboo or palm leaves, vegetable ivory or raspberry jam wood, the economics are the same: If humans can learn to use these materials responsibly, in some cases substituting them for non-renewable alternatives, they will reward us with a sustainable future. Vitale's pictures remind us of the benefits to indigenous populations as well; instead of depleting the lands and waters on which they depend, they can continue to embrace their traditions while gaining a measure of economic stability, if not prosperity. They also raise a question: Can the transit from raw materials in mostly undeveloped places to products marketed in highly developed consumer economies—the dynamic mostly in play here—be sustainably reversed? In other words, can the economic model of colonialism, in which industrial production depends on resources extracted from non-industrialized peoples, flow backward in an age often touted as post-industrial, resulting in benefits to all of us?

The photographs make clear that we do not all have to live in urban centers or work in office and factory buildings to live productive and meaningful lives, and they also tell us that it is possible to live in partnership with the natural world. Of course this is the moral of the story of the design commissions as well. Even if we believe, as some do, that modern photography and design were created to help feed the maw of an emergent consumer economy, there is evidence here that they can teach us to consume not just more but more wisely. Today's generation of designers has taken this brief to heart, thinking of its profession as an ethical endeavor with responsibilities beyond simply making ungainly objects attractive.

Whether photographers share a similar sense of ethical obligation is a matter of debate. Certainly some, like Shubankar Banerjee, Susan Meiselas, Sebastiao Salgado, and Vitale herself, are greatly concerned with the impact of their pictures on the lives of their subjects, using the rhetoric of the image to try to effect social change. But the struggle to change things for the better involves not just the subject, but also the audience of the photograph. How can we change the way we consume photographs so that we have a sustainable relationship with their messages? Too often, it seems, we let camera images wash over us in an unending stream, blithely ignoring the urgency of their messages.

Here, I think, design (thought of in the broadest sense) can come to the rescue. By contextualizing photographs as part of a bigger story, or by making them into material objects in their own right (in the exhibition, some of Vitale's pictures are printed on aluminum shingles), a designer can ensure that we look at them longer, and more deeply, than we look at, say, a computer's screen saver. Conversely, photographs can supply designers with narrative and an added dimension of time, with a before, during, and after on which storytelling depends. Together, design and photography shape our understanding of *Design for a Living World* and of The Nature Conservancy's efficacy in helping preserve diversity in the natural world, which also is the world of human beings.

A group of the spectacular and colorful Urania butterflies on ground in Bolivia.

micronesia

pohnpei, federated states of micronesia

TOP LEFT A cardinal honeyeater sits in a tree in the ancient rock city ruins of Nan Madol on Pohnpei's east coast.

TOP RIGHT A Palau spear fisherman hunts for fish outside Pohnpei's reef. The bounty of Pohnpei's sea and forests has sustained people for hundreds of years.

BOTTOM Twisted mangrove trees shelter birds and provide protection and food for juvenile reef fish in their underwater roots. Here, land and sea are deeply connected: the mangroves' root systems protect coral reefs from sediment and pollution, while the reefs protect the mangroves from the force of waves.

PREVIOUS PAGE Coral reefs, volcanic rocks, and mangrove swamps surround the Micronesian island of Pohnpei.

On the island of Pohnpei, rivers flow through emerald-green forests and tumble in waterfalls down sheer cliffs. Steep mountains soar over turquoise ocean waters, in which angelfish and butterfly fish dart around barrier reefs. Along the shore, land and sea intertwine in the tangle of twisted mangrove forest that encircles the island. These rich resources have sustained Pohnpeians for centuries. Nourished by extraordinary amounts of rain, this rugged place teems with birds, butterflies, lizards, and hundreds of native plants found nowhere else. Everywhere, reminders of Pohnpei's volcanic origins five million years ago abound—from the black basalt rocks jutting into the air to the fertile volcanic soils that nurture forests of breadfruit, banana, coconut, and taro.

In these island forests, the men of Kapinga Village use long poles to harvest fruits hanging high up in the trees, and the women weave fibers from pandanus trees into hairpieces, wall hangings, and sleeping mats. In a communal village "carving hut," men carve wind chimes, necklaces, and other objects out of ivory nut palm seeds. In the surrounding seas, the people of Nukuoro, an outer island of Pohnpei state, cultivate native black-lip pearl oysters and sell the pearls in Pohnpei and Hawaii.

For these islanders, selling handicrafts is more than a traditional pastime—it is a living. But Pohnpei's once plentiful resources are threatened by the overharvesting of mangroves, fish, and other species. Forests are also being cleared for agriculture, speeding the spread of invasive species and causing soils to erode into streams and lagoons and smother coral reefs.

Today, the Kapingamarangi and Nukuorans have developed alternative livelihoods that balance the use and protection of island resources. The Nature Conservancy is encouraging these sustainable economic activities while also providing land-management training and helping design protected area networks that link sea and land. Pohnpei state recently joined four other Micronesian countries in the Micronesia Challenge, a commitment to protect 30 percent of nearshore marine resources and 20 percent of terrestrial resources across Micronesia by 2020. The people of Pohnpei are building a conservation movement and finding innovative solutions that meet both the immediate need for natural resources and the need to preserve them for the future.

vegetable ivory and black pearls

In the early twentieth century, the Kapingamarangi people resettled on Pohnpei Island following disasters that damaged their native island, which was under Japanese rule. Mangrove carving for the tourist trade became the Kapingamarangis' primary source of income. Soon, however, overcultivation damaged the island's mangrove forests. In the 1980s, the Kapingamarangi began carving the seed of the ivory nut palm as an alternative to mangrove.

The ivory nut palm tree is native to the swamp forests of Pohnpei and the other islands of Micronesia. Each tree produces numerous seeds, whose creamy, circular inner core—known as vegetable ivory—ranges in diameter from 2 to 4 inches. The material is extremely hard and, because it has no grain, it does not chip when carved. A vibrant local industry has emerged around making vegetable ivory into jewelry, wind chimes, and other small objects. Over the duration of its life, an ivory nut palm tree produces hundreds of seeds that drop naturally to the ground, allowing them to be sustainably harvested.

Black pearls come from the black-lip oyster (*Pinctada margaritifera*), which is native to many Pacific island reefs. The oyster secretes a pigment that gives its pearls a dark luster ranging from black to gray. Because the oysters can only thrive in extremely clean and healthy lagoons, conservation works hand-in-hand with developing a pearl industry. Because the black-lip oyster lives in relatively remote areas and produces its pearls slowly, over a two-year period, black pearls are more costly than white ones, which are created by more common species of oysters in as few as eight months. Strands of black pearls are extraordinarily expensive because the broad range of colors among the pearls makes matching difficult. Black pearls are cultivated via a seeding process, as the spontaneous occurrence of pearls is extremely rare. So-called "baroque" pearls with an irregular shape are a more viable product for this region, where the pearl industry is just beginning to develop.

ted muehling

BRONZE AND SILVER
CANDLESTICKS, 2008
E. R. Butler & Co.

TORTOISE BOWL, 2006
Hand-cut glass, Steuben

SCARAB EARINGS, 2007
Ted Muehling

In his workshop in downtown Manhattan, Ted Muehling surrounds himself with relics of nature. Feathers, stones, shells, mounted butterflies, and a taxidermic turkey take their place alongside his own works in progress, which range from simple pendant earrings to painted porcelain dishes and bronze candlesticks. Muehling is known for his carefully made, rigorously observed jewelry and objects, whose spare lines are drawn from the natural world. This craftsman is at ease with the intimate tools of the jeweler, working at close range on materials such as gold, silver, natural pearls, and precious stones. Trained as an industrial designer, he has collaborated with manufacturers such as Steuben Glass and Nymphenburg Porcelain, designing objects that are produced according to exacting industrial processes in factories far away from his studio.

Muehling studies natural forms and distills them into a few essential curves and planes. His gently colored teardrop earrings are like swollen beads of dew ready to fall. A crystal bowl for Steuben, inspired by a tortoise shell, is made from a thick ovoid vessel of blown glass that is then cut away with large concave facets, yielding a form that is both geometric and organic and captures and reflects the light around it in simple yet ingeniously organized planes.

For The Nature Conservancy, Muehling traveled to the distant shores of Micronesia to observe the natural beauty of Pohnpei and to learn how native craftspeople carve vegetable ivory. Muehling transformed vegetable ivory and pearls into a series of bracelets, necklaces, and other items that show the beauty of these natural materials.

New York designer Ted Muehling looks for ivory nuts in a forest on Pohnpei. Muehling created a series of jewelry pieces using Micronesian black pearls and vegetable ivory that captures the spirit of this remote Pacific island.

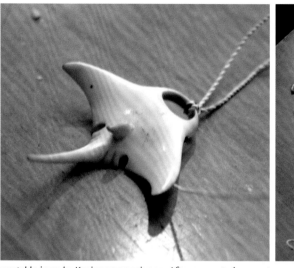

While in Pohnpei, Ted Muehling collected samples of tourist jewelry carved from vegetable ivory by Kapingamarangi men. After encountering manta rays on a

Back in his studio in New York, Muehling took some of the vegetable ivory carvings from Pohnpei and refined the pieces by adding detail work with his jeweler's tools.

To work around imperfections found in the raw material, Muehling carved facets into the jewelry, and in some cases used a blow torch to darken the color.

diving trip, Muehling became interested in one man's carving of a stingray, which he later incorporated into a delicate pair of earrings featuring vegetable ivory.

Muehling strung together a beautiful series of traditionally carved flowers, knotting them on a length of silk cord to create an elegantly spaced lei or garland.

Naturally, vegetable ivory is white, but with his deft application of a torch, Muehling was able to create a a rich, dark color or tortoiseshell effect for his jewelry.

vegetable ivory and black pearl commission

Ted Muehling traveled to the Micronesian island of Pohnpei with The Nature Conservancy. There he met with local craftsmen who create small pendants based on native fish and flowers. He incorporated some of their distinctive carvings into new jewelry pieces that transcend typical tourist wares. For example, Muehling devised a pair of earrings from vegetable ivory carved in the shape of a manta ray; by separating the tail from the wing, he added motion to the pendant's form. Another piece consists of a simple lei made by spacing carved flowers along a silk cord.

Back in his studio in New York, Muehling fashioned a series of cuffs that follow the natural crescent shape of the whole vegetable ivory nut. Because the nuts are often damaged by insects after they fall to the forest floor, Muehling cut facets into the material to remove blemishes while creating an intriguing surface. He also carved nuts into the shape of a shell to make small, elegant containers.

Many of the tools used by the Kapingamarangi men to carve the ivory nut are hand-made from old metal files.

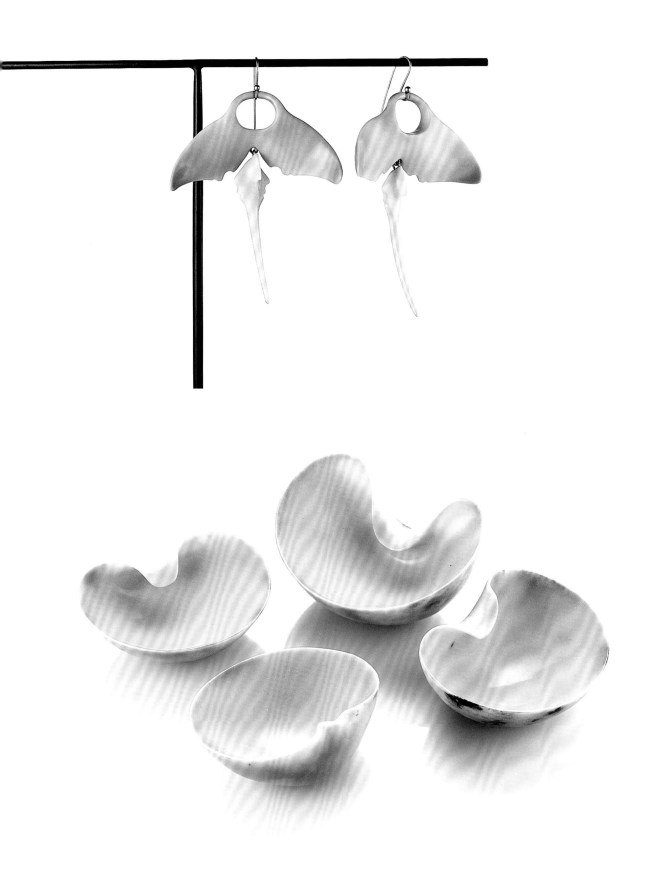

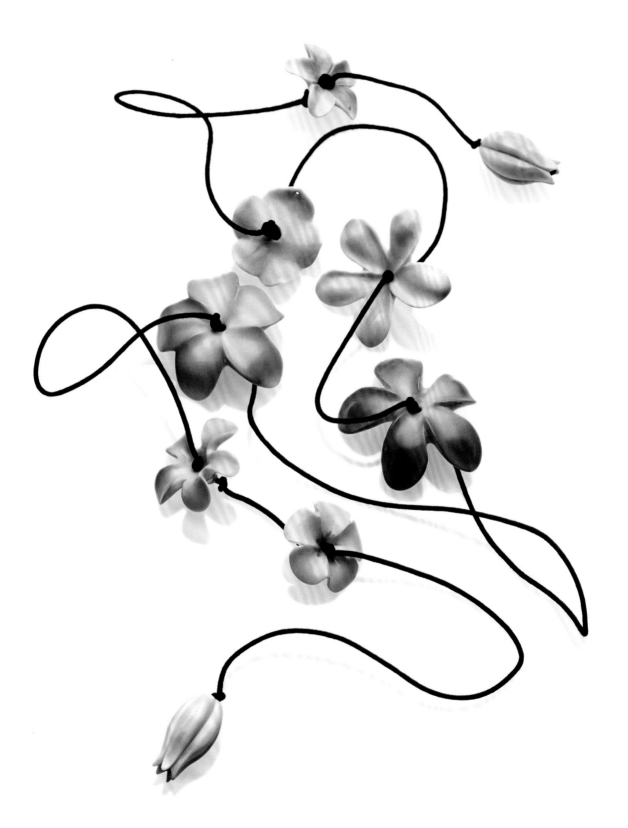

"Whether it's plastic or ivory nut, I love playing with a new material. The nut does beautiful things, unpredictable things. It gets darker at the edges where it starts to oxidize." *Ted Muehling*

SPECIFICATIONS

Dimensions (H X W X D):
page 47: 6.4 X 6.7 X 3.5 CM (2 1/2 X 2 5/8 X 1 3/8 IN.) each

page 48: TOP LEFT: 1 X 2.9 CM (3/8 X 1 1/8 IN.), TOP RIGHT: 5.4 X 6.4 X 1.3 CM (2 1/8 X 2 1/2 X 1/2 IN.), BOTTOM: 15.2 X 12.1 X 0.6 CM (6 X 4 3/4 X 1/4 IN.)

page 49: TOP: 7 X 5.1 X 1.6 CM (2 3/4 X 2 X 5/8 IN.), BOTTOM: 1.9 X 5.7 X 4.8 CM (3/4 X 2 1/4 X 1 7/8 IN.)

page 50: 38.1 X 15.2 X 2.5 CM (15 X 6 X 1 IN.)

Materials: cord, gold, black pearl, vegetable ivory

SOURCING

The pearls used in Ted Muehling's jewelry were purchased from Nukuoro Black Pearls. The tiny atoll of Nukuoro is home to about 300 people and represents one of the most remote communities on Earth. The pearls are formed by black-lip pearl oysters which occur in abundance in Nukuoro's lagoon.

The Caroline ivory nut palm grows in abundance across the islands of Micronesia. The seeds used in this commission were collected mainly from the grounds of the Village Hotel in Pohnpei and prepared by the expert Kapingamarangi carvers. Carved ivory-nut jewelry made in Kapinga Village can be found in gift shops across the Federated States of Micronesia.

SUPPORT

Special thanks to the Conservation Society of Pohnpei, the Village Hotel, the carvers at the Kapinga Village Carving Workshop, the Yela Environmental Landowners Association, the Marshall Island Conservation Society, and Robert Reimers Enterprises, Inc.

Object photography on pages 47–50 by Jay Zukerkorn.

gondwana link, australia

To picture the Gondwana Link landscape of southwestern Australia is to imagine the beautiful, curious, and rare. The trunks of white-barked eucalyptus trees grow underground, their branches rising out of the soil to collect the sparse rainfall. Dramatic scarlet banksias, delicate orchids, and carnivorous plants blanket the earth. Kangaroos hop along lonely dirt roads at dusk. Primordial soils and rocks harbor the earliest traces of life on the planet.

This prehistoric land is one of the most biologically diverse places in the world—nearly ten thousand distinct species exist here. It also holds significant spiritual meaning for Aboriginal peoples like the Noongar and Ngadju, who have lived here for thousands of years. Traditionally, the Noongar continually moved throughout the region, following the availability of food sources. Their reliance on the land is so embedded in their culture that they divide the year into six seasons corresponding to these movements.

European colonization brought disease, violence, and misguided government policies to these people and their natural environment. Aboriginal populations were forcibly removed from their traditional lands as part of an effort to turn the region into Australia's "breadbasket." Aggressive clearing for agriculture drew ancient salts to the surface, leaving large areas barren and inhospitable to native species. Fragmentation, salinity, invasive plants, wildfires, and climate change threaten diversity.

Efforts to heal this land have sparked the most ambitious conservation campaign in Australia's history. The Gondwana Link project—a partnership of leading Australian conservation groups and The Nature Conservancy—seeks to protect, reconnect, and restore 620 miles of bush land across a network of core wilderness areas. The project is acquiring land, establishing conservation easements, and revegetating areas cleared for agriculture.

Equally important is helping indigenous cultures re-establish ancestral connections to the land. Sandalwood, quandong, and raspberry jam wood—important resources for the Noongar and Ngadju—are being planted as part of the restoration effort. By involving the traditional owners in land management decisions, supporting cultural activities, and creating sustainable income opportunities, the project is working to preserve both the cultural and natural legacy of this irreplaceable landscape.

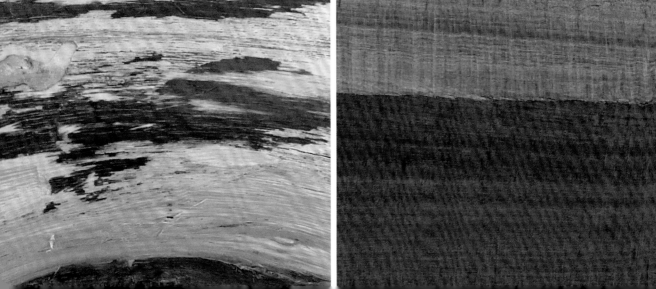

raspberry jam wood

The raspberry jam tree (*Acacia acuminata*) is a small shrub native to Western Australia. The tree gets its curious name from the sweet, fruity smell of its freshly cut limbs. Raspberry jam wood has a deep purplish color and a distinctive visible grain. It is commonly used for fence posts because of the material's extreme hardness and density, as well as its ready-to-use scale. Fences found throughout the Gondwana Link area have a gnarly, prehistoric character, and the wood's exterior becomes silvery gray over time. Cutting through one of these exposed, weathered limbs, however, reveals the material's richly colored core.

Raspberry jam is a primary host for sandalwood, a small parasitic tree that is highly valued for its aromatic oil. Sandalwood has shallow roots and depends on other trees and shrubs for its own survival. Because of the plant's parasitic nature, sandalwood plantations are intrinsically biodiverse, as each tree must grow among a cluster of other plants, including raspberry jam.

Restoring native vegetation like the raspberry jam and sandalwood trees is critical to battling the salinity that plagues the region. When large swaths of land were cleared for agriculture in the twentieth century, thirsty, deep-rooted native plants were replaced with shallow rooted, less thirsty ones, causing the water table to rise. Salt deposits were thus drawn to the surface, leaving behind salt lakes and toxic soil.

Populating the area with native trees makes it a vibrant place where both wildlife and people flourish. The Noongar people, who were forcibly removed from the bush to make way for agriculture, are now reconnecting to the rural landscape and finding ways to make a living from it.

stephen burks

CK N2U, 2007
Fragrance packaging

PARALLEL, 2005
Shelving

TATU, 2007
Wire side tables and
seating

A product designer whose career encompasses interiors, exhibitions, and products, Stephen Burks actively engages with the users and makers of his work as well as with materials and techniques. From his base in New York City, he has collaborated with international manufacturers and local businesses to create objects and environments that are a pleasure to look at and use, as well as socially beneficial.

Burks created his TaTu objects for Artecnica's Design with a Conscience program. Artecnica, a product-development company, paired leading designers with artisans in different parts of the world to create products that celebrate craft, fair trade, local creativity, and sustainable materials and manufacturing. TaTu is a collection of steel-wire objects, hand-woven by artisans in South Africa, that disassemble and reassemble to form tables, trays, stools, and open vessels. Burks also worked with South African craftspeople via Aid to Artisans, an organization that connects artisan groups with the global marketplace.

Burks continued this line of inquiry with his Love collection of silicone bowls for Cappellini. Women in South Africa produce these bowls, which are inlaid with ceramic tiles, using a proprietary process invented by Burks. In a more playful vein, his Patchwork vases for Missoni are covered with reclaimed remnants of the company's signature fabrics and adhered with resin to existing vessels to create high-touch artifacts with raucous visual appeal.

The Nature Conservancy invited Burks to visit Australia and observe how the Noongar people interact with the landscape of the Gondwana Link.

New York industrial
designer Stephen Burks
refines his drawings
of a prototype he
designed that is made
from raspberry jam
wood, a tree native to
southwestern Australia.

Stephen Burks traveled to southwest Australia and met with members of the Noongar Aboriginal group, who have lived in the region for thousands of years.

Native plants and trees such as raspberry jam wood and quandong continue to be used in Noongar daily life. In an effort to create new, sustainable livelihoods,

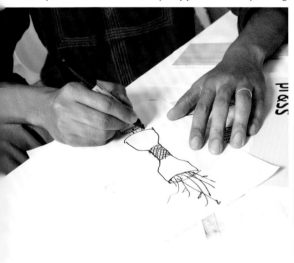

Back in his studio in New York, Burks was inspired by his gathering trips in the bush and was impressed with the dark, rich tones of raspberry jam wood. He created a

The Gondwana Link project has helped bring back the land from depleted agricultural fields to a diverse and complex mosaic of plant and animal species.

the Noongar are exploring innovative uses of these materials through an organic skin-care line. Burks accompanied Noongar leaders on a tour through the bush.

piece carved from jam wood that allows for the collection and processing of plant-based materials for use in a variety of lotions, salves, and other products.

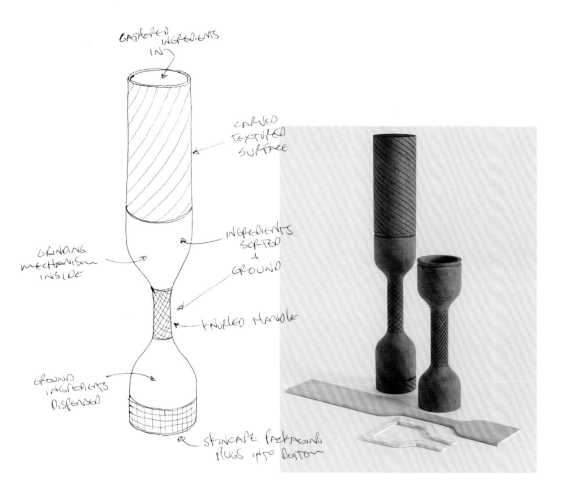

rasberry jam wood commission

Stephen Burks calls his project a "three-dimensional diagram" of the Noongar process of gathering plant essences (seeds, nuts, berries, twigs, and such) in the bush for therapeutic or medicinal purposes. He created a conceptual prototype for an object that integrates the process of gathering and grinding plant materials. Specimens are collected in the top container, ground in the handle, and dispensed from the bottom, where the material can be processed again to create lotions, oils, and other products.

The Noongars are working to develop an organic skin-care line using raw materials harvested from the recently reclaimed land at Nowanup. Burks's totem includes a packaging prototype for the Noongars' products. "My totem piece is like a nomadic apothecary for crushing materials by hand," explains Burks. "Conceptually, the object is an interim step between the field and the home lab, where essences are processed into final products. I wanted to manifest that process in an object. It is a physical tool, but also a kind of spiritual tool."

Burks's drawings (left) and early prototype (right) demonstrate how his piece transforms raw, organic materials into a final product.

"I sought to connect to the Noongar tradition of gathering these natural ingredients for their healing properties, and then further connect to the contemporary transformation of those ingredients into a real product." *Stephen Burks*

SPECIFICATIONS

Dimensions (H x W x D): pages 63–66: 57.5 X 10.2 CM (22 5/8 X 4 IN.)

Materials: bath salts, lotion, metal, plastic, quandong seeds, raspberry jam wood, soap

SOURCING

Stephen Burks's commissioned piece was carved from fence posts collected by Margi Weir of Greening Australia from a former farm in Western Australia. The raspberry jam wood fence posts were dismantled as part of the Gondwana Link reclamation effort. The cosmetics were made and provided by the Noongar Aboriginal Group in partnership with the Gondwana Link Project. The raspberry jam wood prototypes were carved by Richard Newton.

SUPPORT

Special thanks to Keith Bradby, Bush Heritage, Greening Australia, and the traditional owners of Gondwana Link —the Noongar people whom The Nature Conservancy acknowledges as the original inhabitants of the land.

Object photography on pages 62–66 by Dan Whipps.

costa rica

la amistad international park, costa rica

TOP A cable bridge crosses the Río Tsqui River. The indigenous Bribri people have lived in this pocket of rainforest in La Amistad International Park for centuries.

BOTTOM LEFT A Bribri man collects cacao seeds inside a banana leaf in the village of Yorkin, situated near the border of Costa Rica and Panama. Cacao is the name of the tree and pods, while cocoa describes the seeds and products made from the seeds.

BOTTOM RIGHT Although Costa Rica covers only 0.01 percent of the earth's landmass, it is believed to host approximately 5 percent of its biological diversity. Pictured here is a boat-billed heron.

PREVIOUS PAGE A young boy takes the fruit from a cacao tree in Costa Rica, which is sacred to the Bribri community.

Tucked away in the southeastern corner of Costa Rica, the fog-shrouded cloud forests and cascading rivers of La Amistad International Park remain one of the largest, least-disturbed areas in Central America.

Deep within this remote, mountainous wilderness, worn dirt paths wind through twisted trees and lead to a small community of the indigenous Bribri people. Resplendent quetzals and great green macaws fly through the forest canopy, while pumas, giant anteaters, ocelots, and peccaries roam the blanket of mosses, ferns, and orchids covering the ground. The mellow, rich smell of roasting cocoa beans floats through the village as children play in a nearby river and men cast fishing nets.

Using their ancient knowledge of cacao cultivation, the women of this community pooled their land and resources to form an organic-chocolate cooperative. By working as a collective, they are earning more money for their cocoa and chocolate products than on their own. Together, the women handpick large yellow pods, dry the beans in the sun or in a drying machine, and package them for export to Europe. Others turn the beans into thick chocolate that is sold locally.

Community-based cooperatives like this create economic stability in one of the poorest areas of Costa Rica. By offering sustainable, alternative livelihoods, they also alleviate the serious threats facing La Amistad: development, incompatible agricultural activities, and unregulated hunting. Because the delicate cacao trees thrive in the shade and protection of larger trees, cacao cultivation relies on a healthy forest. And by using organic methods, this women's cooperative is avoiding harmful chemicals that can contaminate the air and water.

The Nature Conservancy has helped seventeen community groups in La Amistad come together as a network known as Red Indígena de Turismo. Through the network, members receive training and resources to develop environmentally friendly economic activities like ecotourism as well as sustainable agricultural practices. Empowering local people through this network creates viable income opportunities while preserving indigenous culture and the spec-tacular lands of La Amistad—one of Costa Rica's last natural frontiers.

cocoa

TOP Cacao seeds ripen inside the fruit, where fungus starts a fermentation process that raises the temperature in the fruit up to 50 degrees centigrade. The bean changes from purple to brown and is ready for harvesting after five days.

BOTTOM LEFT A buyer checks the quality of a fermented cocoa bean by cutting it in half and inspecting the inside.

BOTTOM RIGHT It is believed that the Mayans and Aztecs brewed cacao with vanilla, chili, and pepper. The beans were so precious that they were used as a currency by the Aztecs.

Cocoa beans come from the tree Theobroma cacao, which grows in many tropical regions. The Mayans began cultivating the cacao tree for human use thousands of years ago. Today, chocolate—which is made by combining roasted, ground cocoa seeds with sugar, vanilla, and other ingredients—is a huge global industry. To meet the global demand for chocolate, cocoa farmers clear-cut rainforests in West Africa and elsewhere, establishing plantations that vastly reduce biological diversity.

The cacao tree thrives best in shade, under the protective canopy of taller fruit trees, mahogany trees, and other shade plants. These shade trees, which shield the pods from wind and sun while helping the soil retain moisture, are valuable in themselves and can be sustainably grown and harvested. Although rustic cocoa cultivation takes place in indigenous forest growth, most cocoa farmers use planted shade trees to some extent. A diverse forest supports an array of animal life, including bats and wasps that feed on the pests that damage cacao trees. Cocoa farming demonstrates the interdependence of biodiversity and healthy crop yield. It is a highly successful form of agroforestry, in which crops are raised within a forest setting.

Women in La Amistad grow and process cocoa beans for export as well as for local use. One product sold in nearby markets is a handmade cocoa patty, enjoyed at celebratory occasions such as births and weddings. Shavings from the patty are sprinkled into hot milk or water to make a festive chocolate beverage. Yves Béhar's packaging of this community-based product aims to allow access to a wider market and stimulate demand for a less-processed form of the beloved substance.

yves béhar

ALIPH JAWBONE, 2008
Headset

XOXO, 2008
Laptop

Yves Béhar rocketed to prominence at the turn of the twenty-first century, becoming one of the world's leading industrial designers. After founding the product design and branding company fuseproject in San Francisco in 1999, the Swiss-born Béhar quickly attracted some of the world's most savvy and influential clients, from high-tech giants like Toshiba and Hewlett-Packard to the counterculture icon Birkenstock and the fashion iconoclast Hussein Chalayan.

Whether creating a crystal chandelier or a wireless headset, Béhar pays close attention to details and materials. He also places primary value on human experience and actively seeks ways to improve public health and welfare through design. Among his most influential designs is a laptop created in partnership with Nicholas Negroponte and the One Laptop Per Child program. This global initiative brought together the power of design, technology, industry, and governments to give children in developing countries better access to education via computers and Internet connectivity. Creating several iterations of the laptop, Béhar tackled major challenges in manufacturing and networking while yielding a playful and approachable object.

As a gift to New York City, Béhar created a user-friendly, fashion-forward condom dispenser for the city's health department. The condom package plays on the city's distinctive transit signage, while the dispenser sports an easy-to-maintain design that makes it appealing to end users as well as to the bars, restaurants, and public organizations that put it on display.

The Nature Conservancy commissioned Béhar to visit Costa Rica and look at local traditions for growing, harvesting, processing, and consuming cocoa, one of the most prized products of the region's rainforest. Béhar approached the project from his integral design philosophy, devising a solution that embraces branding, packaging, and the user experience while celebrating the sheer beauty of well-made things.

Swiss industrial designer Yves Béhar sketches designs in his studio in New York. Béhar traveled to Costa Rica and met with a women's organic chocolate cooperative.

Organic cocoa farming requires a diverse habitat because the cocoa tree thrives under forest cover. Since 2005, cocoa has been produced in the forested highlands

To make cocoa, the women hand-pick the cacao pods, dry the beans, roast and grind them, and add sugar, vanilla, and other ingredients.

For celebratory occasions, such as a wedding or birth of a baby, the women create a beverage by shaping the cocoa into patties that are shaved into cups of hot milk.

of the Talamanca Mountains in La Amistad International Park by seventy indigenous women who pooled their resources to form an organic chocolate cooperative.

Some of the beans are roasted in a small factory in the area and then shipped to Europe to be made into chocolate.

The beans are shipped in jute bags, which inspired the packaging for Béhar's own design. Béhar designed a simple, elegant tool that is used to shave the cocoa patties.

cocoa commission

When Béhar visited Costa Rica to meet with the women's organic chocolate association supported by The Nature Conservancy, he was struck by the local custom of preparing hot chocolate from patties of hand-processed cocoa. In response, Béhar created a tool for preparing and enjoying this traditional beverage. The beautifully crafted implement is designed for scraping bits of cocoa off the larger patty; the cocoa shavings collect inside the hollow tool, and when the user turns the instrument over, the cocoa falls into a cup. Hot milk or water is added, and the beverage is stirred.

Béhar's sketches demonstrate how his instrument is to be used to create the traditional Bribri chocolate beverage.

Béhar's design also includes a cloth bag made from jute that holds the cocoa patty. Instructions for using the tool and preparing the drink are printed on the bag. If produced, this project would broaden the potential market for this local product. "I hope someone will pick up on the commercial potential of this project," says Béhar. "This is the first step toward a modest solution that could function well for this particular community."

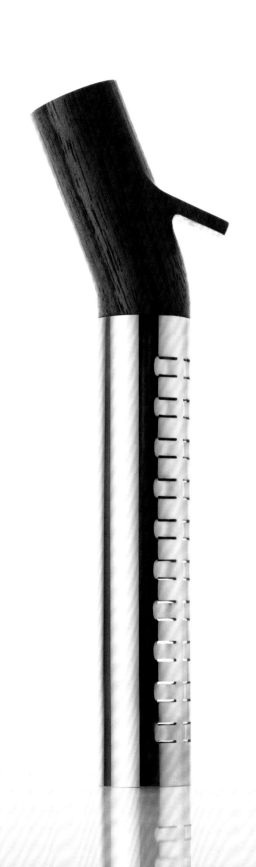

"We walked into what looked like a forest, but actually it was somebody's farm. Palms, banana trees, and cacao trees were all mixed together, where they protect one another.... We designed a product that celebrates the process of preparing cocoa. The design is simple and elegant but also primitive and ritualistic." *Yves Béhar*

SPECIFICATIONS

Dimensions (H X W X D):
pages 79–82:
14 X 3.2 X 1.9 CM
(5 1/2 X 1 1/4 X 3/4 IN.)

Materials: aluminum, burlap, cocoa, hardwood, rope

SOURCING

Cocoa featured in Yves Béhar's commission was made by the Asociacion Comision de Mujeres Indigenas Brisbris de Talamanca (ACOMUITA), an organic cocoa cooperative managed by women from the Bribri community on the Caribbean side of Costa Rica. ACOMUITA income comes from tours of chocolate production and sales of chocolate products locally, as well as sales to the Asociación de Pequeños Productores de Talamanca (APPTA), a Costa Rican organization with more than 1,000 members that sells organic cocoa beans to the international market. The cocoa tool and packaging prototypes were made in California by Sputnick Models.

SUPPORT

Special thanks to the Asociación de Pequeños Productores de Talamanca (APPTA), Asociación Comisión de Mujeres Indígenas Bribris de Talamanca (ACOMUITA), Estibrawpa, Finca Educativa, Red Indígena de Turismo, and Steven DeVries from DeVries Chocolate.

Object photography on pages 78, 80–82 by Dan Whipps. Object photography on page 79 by Jay Zukerkorn.

bolivia

santa cruz, bolivia

TOP The sprawling landscape of southern Bolivia is composed of many poor towns. Most homes have little access to running water and do not have electricity. Though they may lack financial wealth, the towns boast rich baroque music traditions.

BOTTOM Alejandra Pavisich speaks with workers living in the remote forests outside of Cururú, Bolivia, about their sustainable forest management program.

PREVIOUS PAGE The Uribicha Orchestra waits inside a Jesuit church during the Baroque Music Festival in San Xavier, Bolivia. The orchestra has traveled to other countries to perform; in 2003, it won the 13th Bartolomé de las Casas award in recognition of its efforts to preserve the artistic and musical heritage of the Jesuit missions.

Hundreds of miles from the dry Chiquitano forests of eastern Bolivia, Santa Cruz hums with the sounds of a fast-growing, multicultural city. Modern buildings stand beside Spanish colonial churches—visible reminders of the history that helped shape the city and country. Today, Bolivia has a new legacy as one of the world leaders in FSC-certified (Forest Stewardship Council) tropical forests.

Fifteen years ago, Bolivia's unregulated forestry industry left forests depleted of precious wood species, and there was little hope they could be sustained. In 2003, The Nature Conservancy began working on a project with the Bolivian government and the U.S. Agency for International Development (USAID) to promote sustainable-forest-management principles. Through this project, the Conservancy has provided technical assistance to companies seeking certification and is linking FSC-certified companies like CIMAL (Compañía Maderera Ltda.) to potential export markets.

Through FSC certification, forest-management practices are evaluated by an independent third party according to economic, environmental, and social standards. From its origins in forests near indigenous communities to finished products on store shelves, wood is tracked through the supply chain into the marketplace, where businesses and consumers can choose wood and paper products that are harvested legally and responsibly.

The Conservancy works to increase the supply of and demand for FSC-certified forest products worldwide. In Bolivia, CIMAL and other companies have been successful in expanding the global marketplace for certified products. Increased demand, in turn, has led to the certification of almost 5 million acres of Bolivia's forestland—nearly one-quarter of the country's managed forests. As the demand for FSC certification grows both nationally and internationally, Bolivia's forestry industry can also continue to expand, while its forests become stronger and healthier.

MADERA
FSC-PURO

fsc-certified plywood

In the manufacture of plywood, water softens the log before it is peeled into thin veneers or "plies," which are then glued together with the grains running in opposite directions. Plywood's cross-grain, multilayered construction yields a strong, flat, consistent material that resists warping and cracking. Higher-quality veneers from more valuable, slower-growing trees are commonly used for the outer surface, while less costly material from faster-growing trees is used inside.

Bolivian plywood is made from seven different trees, including yesquero blanco, amargo, and bibosi. The forests of Bolivia—which are some of the largest on Earth—provide a rich habitat for countless species while helping to protect the world's climate by absorbing huge amounts of carbon. These forests have long been threatened by shortsighted logging practices. Private timber companies invade the forests in search of valuable trees such as mahogany, scarring the land with roads and leaving behind a barren, fragmented landscape. The loggers take their profits and go, while the communities that once depended on the forest are left with a battered and polluted landscape exposed to erosion and species extinction.

BOLFOR II (Bolivian Sustainable Forestry Project II) is an enormous forest-protection plan launched by the Bolivian government and USAID. The project, coordinated by The Nature Conservancy, trains local communities and businesses to sustainably extract from the forest while encouraging public investment in forest protection and promoting the use of sustainable forest products. As a result, incomes have improved for participating communities, and millions of acres have been successfully protected. BOLFOR II has also helped Bolivia participate more fully in the global economy.

Today, 125 different species of trees are being sustainably harvested in Bolivia, bringing increased prosperity to local communities in a country where two-thirds of the population lives in poverty. Growing demand for certified sustainable wood products in Europe and the United States is yielding higher prices for the people of Bolivia and building incentives to protect the country's life-giving forests.

abbott miller

THE COUCH, 2006
The Sigmund Freud
Museum, Vienna

ENGINE TOWER, 2003
Harley-Davidson
Open Road Tour

VILLAGE WORKS, 1999

Abbott Miller experiments
with how alternative textile
elements might connect
to the frame of the chair.
Stringing a measuring
tape through the chair
allowed him to see how
much material is required
to lace the chair from
a continuous length of
cotton webbing.

Abbott Miller's design practice bridges two- and three-dimensional design. While he works primarily as a graphic designer, he has developed a specialization in the hybrid world of exhibition design, often transposing the flatness of graphics into three-dimensional forms. His earliest forays into exhibitions were projects in which he also served as an author and curator, giving him a unique understanding of how to use texts, images, and objects to tell stories. His curatorial projects—which have included topics on design, art, and social history—bring an editorial mind and a designer's eye to the problem of creating dramatic environments that encourage interaction and interpretation.

His collaborations with curators and museums have included a number of innovative exhibitions, including *The Couch: Thinking in Repose* at The Sigmund Freud Museum in Vienna, which used Freud's apartment building for a site-specific exhibition examining the role of the couch in psychoanalysis. Miller's design inserted a false floor that treated the exhibition space as an archaeological site, embodying one of Freud's dominant metaphors of psychoanalysis. Drawing from motifs within the building, a meandering rivulet of ornament mounted to the ceiling guided visitors through a labyrinth of rooms.

Miller and his design team also created the permanent exhibitions for the new Harley-Davidson Museum in Milwaukee—a follow-up to his international traveling Open-Road Tour, which featured circus-size tents emblazoned with enormous letters and a tower built from three-dimensional letterforms. Many of Miller's projects find inspiration in the architecture of letterforms. An early exhibition and book called *Dimensional Typography*, which looked at how letters become three-dimensional, has served as a touchstone for many of Miller's environmental projects.

Miller's project for this exhibition looks at how forms plotted on a plane of FSC-certified plywood can yield a distinctive chair design. The organic forms of mid-century modernism are translated into a graphic composition that, once cut, is dry-assembled into a sculptural whole.

Carpenters at Kaoba, a successful furniture factory in Santa Cruz, use a broad variety of Bolivian hardwoods, veneers, and plywood. The carpenters use

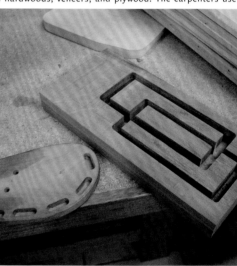

A trade school in Santa Cruz is equipped with a sophisticated CNC router, which is used to produce furniture, as well as provide training to students. Vernacular

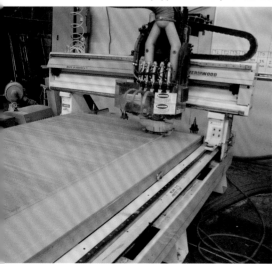
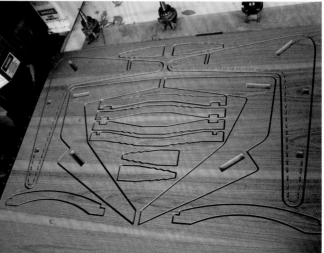

Three chairs are routed from one sheet of plywood. Holes cut into the frame of the chair allow the textile, the seat, and back to be held in tension,

traditional carpentry to produce both historical and modern designs for the Bolivian market and for export.

patterns, weaving traditions, as well as the use of CNC routing, inspired Miller and his colleague Brian Raby, to create a chair using FSC-certified plywood.

laced from a continuous band of woven cotton webbing.

fsc plywood commission

Abbott Miller and his colleague Brian Raby traveled to Santa
Cruz, Bolivia, to see how the local furniture industry is using
FSC-certified wood harvested from Bolivia's vast, managed forests.
The manufacturers are primarily using hardwoods and traditional
carpentry to provide high-quality design for the domestic market
and for export. Infocal, a local trade school in Santa Cruz, has
been using a sophisticated CNC-milling (computer numerically
controlled) router to increase the efficiencies in its production of
tables, chairs, and desks for schools and organizations in Bolivia.
Miller and Raby were intrigued by the idea of bridging the high-end,
hardwood carpentry they observed with the more utilitarian design
being produced by Infocal. Their chair design exploits the beauty
of Bolivian jatoba wood, while also yielding three chairs per sheet of
plywood with a minimal amount of waste. The components of the
chair can be shipped flat and dry-assembled with a rubber mallet.
The design can be economically produced in Bolivia at Infocal.

Early sketches for the
chair design were based
directly on the exhibition
furniture that Miller
and Raby had created for
displaying artifacts.

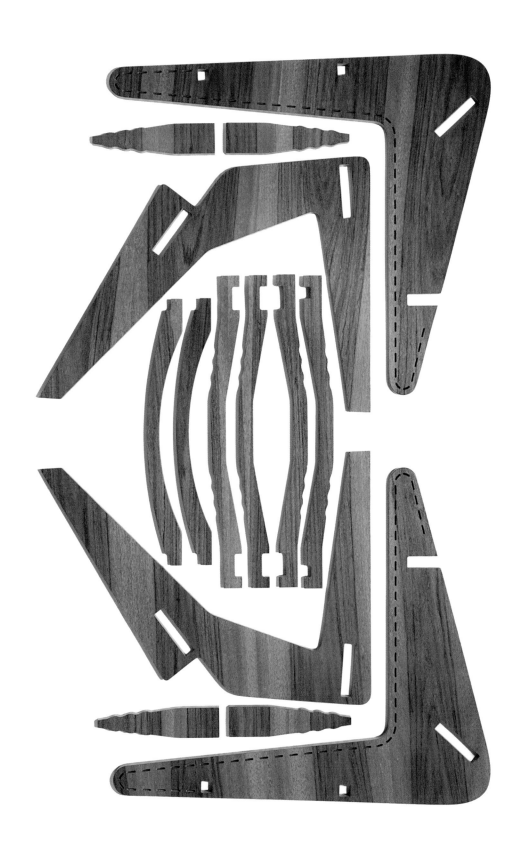

"We were inspired by the astounding variety and beauty of Bolivian woods that we saw, but also by the ingenuity of the vernacular design and architecture in Santa Cruz. The strong traditions of woodworking show through in the factories we visited as well as in the adaptation of CNC routing to the needs of making furniture." *Abbott Miller*

SPECIFICATIONS

Dimensions (H X W X D):
pages 95–98:
86.4 X 52.7 X 55.9 CM
(34 X 20 3/4 X 22 IN.)

Materials: FSC-certified plywood, with an applied veneer of jatoba. 1/2 IN cotton webbing made from 100% cotton.

SOURCING

Jatoba veneer provided by Herzog Veneers Inc. (Ted Bodea provided laminating services out of Greenpoint, Brooklyn). CNC routing and production provided by Associated Fabrication, Brooklyn. Cotton webbing was sourced from Shaker Workshops.

SUPPORT

Special thanks to Richard Newton, Pablo Pinell, Kaoba Furniture, and Nicomedes Cueto Davila, the director of the trade school Infocal (National Institute for Labour Training).

Object photography on pages 95–98 by Jay Zukerkorn.

guarayo indigenous lands, bolivia

At the core of central Bolivia's lowlands, the moist Amazonian rainforest gently gives way to the drier, thorny scrub forests that characterize southeastern Bolivia. Here, in the transitional Chiquitano Dry Forest, the indigenous Guarayo people have lived off the region's rivers and forests since precolonial times.

High in the palm trees that surround the Guarayo community of Cururú, blue and yellow macaws reveal themselves with bright flashes of color among the treetops. These orchid-laden forests are also home to jaguar and endangered forest tortoise. They are also an important source of food and wood for the Guarayo, whose centuries-old tradition of local woodcarving can be seen in the exquisite mission churches scattered throughout the region.

Today, the Guarayo carve and produce a wide array of wood products, including violins, boats, and household furniture. However, their traditional way of life and the health of these forests are threatened by the expansion of agriculture—especially large-scale soybean production—and illegal and haphazard logging. Road construction is bringing newcomers to the area and fueling urbanization. Small rural communities are under increasing pressure to convert their forests for agriculture or sell their land.

Yet in Cururú and fifteen other Bolivian communities, a more balanced way of life is taking root. Through a project created by the Bolivian government and the U.S. Agency for International Development, Cururú commercially harvests forest resources using sustainable forest management principles. As leader of the project, The Nature Conservancy is working with its partners to provide hands-on technical assistance and training to help local people profitably run a community-forestry enterprise and sustainably manage their forests. Products from wood harvested in Cururú are then shipped to national and international markets bearing the FSC seal of certification.

Since assistance to these community-based enterprises began, local forestry incomes have risen and deforestation rates have declined. Families participating in fourteen different community-forestry enterprises across Bolivia have seen an average 23 percent increase in their income from forestry management over two years. And communities like Cururú are gaining the skills and tools to profit from their rich resources while preserving them for the future.

morado and jipijapa

Communities of artisans in the San Ignacio region of Bolivia work with materials from the forest to create products for local use and sale to the tourist trade. Taller Bolivia, in San Miguel, is a workshop that uses FSC-certified wood. FSC is the fastest growing forest-certification program in the world. Products that bear the FSC logo are certified to have come from a responsibly managed forest. Owned and operated by local artisans, Taller Bolivia produces objects and ornaments that draw on Bolivia's long history of woodcarving. Made from *morado*, or Bolivian rosewood, the carvings are typically varnished or finished in bright colors, but they also can be treated minimally to reveal the natural grain and color of the wood.

The bags commissioned for this project feature elements carved from morado as well as surfaces woven from cotton and *jipijapa*, a fiber made from palm leaves. The cotton is woven by hand in the remote village of Salvatierra, which also manages a community forest. Jipijapa is harvested, processed, and woven into bags and other objects by a collective of women artisans living in the village of Galilea. After cutting leaves from palm trees with machetes, the women boil them with lemon and sulfur to bleach the fibers. They dry the fibers in the sun, boil the leaves again, and dye them in shared vats of color. Dyeing is planned in stages as colors are added to the pot, one by one, to yield a variety of hues.

The workshops, which pursue traditional craft techniques alongside increasingly modern business practices, seek a broader market for their goods. Although the artisans have developed effective means to cooperatively make products with sustainable forest materials, they lack effective means of distribution. Working with designers and importers in the United States and Europe is a way to raise demand for the community's skills and products.

kate spade new york

LIMITED EDITION TOTE
for kate spade store in
Mission Viejo, California

WOMEN FOR WOMEN
Mittens and hat

kate spade was founded in 1993 with an initial line of crisp, geometric handbags constructed from satin-finished nylon that sparked an instant sensation in the cluttered world of fashion accessories. The firm, which now employs dozens of designers devoted to product development, quickly expanded to create shoes, luggage, glasses, paper goods, housewares, and more. Each object in this diverse range of lifestyle products reflects the kate spade signature, which seeks to incorporate modern luxury with a flash of subtle humor.

kate spade has a history of working for social causes. Since 2006, the company has created products in collaboration with Women for Women International, an organization that helps women living in war-torn regions recover from financial and emotional hardship by providing support, training, human rights education, employment opportunities, access to capital, and assistance in small business development. Collaborating with designers at kate spade, survivors of war in Bosnia and Herzegovina hand-knitted a series of clever, graphically driven designs for hats and mittens. Profits are returned to the women through the foundation.

The Nature Conservancy worked with the kate spade design team to develop products in concert with craftspeople in Bolivia. Paulina Reyes, a designer for kate spade and a native of Mexico City, traveled to Bolivia to take the lead on developing a series of woven handbags using morado wood, handwoven cotton, and jipijapa. A limited number of bags will be manufactured for sale in the United States.

Paulina Reyes, a
designer for kate spade,
worked with artisans
in Bolivia.

Scattered about the Chiquitania region of Bolivia are beautifully carved Jesuit mission churches that date back to the late 17th and early 18th centuries.

kate spade designer Paulina Reyes traveled to the region and worked with carvers from the Brothers Guasase workshop, a family business run by five brothers.

Reyes also worked with women from the Association of Artisans of Galilea to experiment with weaving techniques using jipijapa. To make jipijapa, the women cut, boil,

The region is well-known for its commercially valuable tropical hardwood. Beautiful and intricate wood carving still thrives in many small villages today.

Wooden handles were carved from locally grown, FSC-certified hardwood. Reyes also selected hand-carved wooden tiles to embellish a woven cotton handbag.

and bleach palm leaves and then dry them in the sun. The fibers are boiled again, dyed, and finally woven into various objects.

  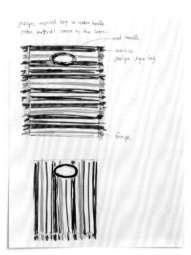

jipijapa and morado commission

While in Bolivia, the kate spade designer Paulina Reyes collaborated with carvers to develop designs for handbags using indigenous materials and techniques. In one prototype, hand-carved wooden tiles are stitched to a cotton fabric understructure. The simple, symmetrical carvings are finished with oil to protect the wood without substantially changing its color.

Another series of bags is made from jipijapa. The finely woven bags have a beautiful diagonal grain. In one design, delicate stripes emphasize the direction of the weave. Round wooden handles are sewn directly to the bags; the large visible stitches provide both a structural connection and graphic interest. The whole process was one of collaboration and mutual exchange. The artisans taught Reyes how to carve and weave, while Reyes showed them new ways to apply their skills. "For me, the best experience was to come from a different place and work with them on what they're used to doing," explains Reyes.

The kate spade designs incorporate FSC-certified, hand-carved morado wood as well as colorfully dyed jipijapa and cotton.

"The structure of the team as far as production goes is way more developed than distribution. These talented craftspeople are spending a lot of time creating things that there might not be a market for, such as woven fans. We hope that by promoting the fact that these communities are doing this work with sustainable materials, this project will help create interest from people who can help with distribution."
Paulina Reyes, kate spade new york

SPECIFICATIONS

Dimensions (H X W X D):
page 111: 33 X 36.8 X 2.5 CM (13 X 14 1/2 X 1 IN.)

page 112: 37.5 X 26.7 X 2.5 CM (14 3/4 X 10 1/2 X 1 IN.)

page 113: 33 X 36.8 X 2.5 CM (13 X 14 1/2 X 1 IN.)

page 114: 33 X 43.2 X 2.5 CM (13 X 17 X 1 IN.)

Materials: jipijapa (palm leaf), morado (Bolivian hardwood), and cotton

SOURCING

The cotton fabric was woven by hand by the artisans of Salvatierra, a remote village in Bolivia that also manages a community forest. Salvatierra is known for its high-quality, long-lasting, and colorful hammocks. The carved tiles, made from FSC-certified morado wood, were made by the skilled carvers at Taller Hermanos Guasase (Brother Guasase), a family-owned workshop in San Ignacio de Velasco, in the Chiquitania region of Bolivia. Taller Guasase uses mission-era carving techniques, which can be seen in the Jesuit churches built there in the eighteenth century. The jipijapa was prepared and woven by artisans in the village of Galilea, who typically make fans and the famous Panama hat from the palm fiber.

SUPPORT

Special thanks to Kristen Evans of Salvatierra Imports, Claudia Mercado, and the artisans of Salvatierra, Taller Hermanos Guasase, and the Association of Artisans of Galilea.

Object photography on pages 110–14 by Dan Whipps.

southwest alaska

Throughout the summer, millions of red, silver, and pink salmon flood the rivers and streams of the Nushagak-Mulchatna watershed in southwest Alaska. Furiously fighting the current, some leap out of the water; others are no more than a flash racing by. It is an epic journey as old as the land itself: from the rivers where they are born, out into the open ocean, and back again to their natal streams to spawn.

These wild salmon are at the heart of all that is Alaska: its people, economy, culture, and wildlife. Brown bears, bald eagles, and otters feast on their abundance. Sport fishermen and commercial fishing boats—part of an industry that provides 47 percent of the state's private-sector jobs—converge on rivers and streams. Native people, who once celebrated the return of salmon with elaborate ceremonies, still net and dry salmon much as they did thousands of years ago. Today, echoes of these traditional celebrations survive in Alaska Native salmon stories and contemporary art.

As one of the last strongholds for wild salmon, Alaska is vulnerable to the same threats that have decimated salmon elsewhere. The Nushagak-Mulchatna watershed is the region's largest, least-protected area of biological significance. Increased recreational use and potential large-scale gold and copper mining threaten to alter river flows and water quality. Climate change can affect the ability of salmon to migrate, spawn, and rear.

Working with various partners and Native villages, The Nature Conservancy uses strategies like acquisitions and conservation easements to protect the watershed. The recent purchase on a tributary of the Mulchatna River benefited landowners by providing a cash sale, preserving traditional access, and protecting vital habitat. The Conservancy is also documenting Native knowledge of the land to develop a plan for the watershed that maintains traditional subsistence activities.

Each season, a seemingly infinite number of salmon begin the perilous journey home to spawn. But as worldwide salmon populations decrease, the need to preserve these remaining healthy wild-salmon runs becomes all the more pressing—for salmon as well as for the people and wildlife that rely on these magnificent fish for their survival.

salmon leather

TOP LEFT Salmon skin comes in a variety of hues: pinks, reds, silvers. However, when it is turned into leather, its natural, undyed color is ivory.

TOP RIGHT A brown bear catches a king salmon at Brooks Falls. Salmon are considered a "keystone species" and are one of the first species to suffer when stream water quality declines.

BOTTOM The Nushagak River has the third largest Chinook run in the country and contributes to the world's largest sockeye run, in Bristol Bay.

For thousands of years, human beings have used leather to create clothing, tools, and shelter. While the modern leather industry relies largely on the skins of animals that are hunted or farmed only for their hides, fish processors discard enormous amounts of potentially valuable material each year as a byproduct of the food industry. Over the past decade, salmon skin has been rediscovered as a beautiful and economically viable product. In Europe, for example, where the leather-goods industry has struggled with tight supplies of basic raw materials, fish canneries and smoking plants can now offer a reliable, affordable source of leather for use in shoes, belts, bags, furnishings, and even bikinis. Sometimes known as "sea leather," this material is also produced elsewhere in the United States as well as Canada, India, South America, and other parts of the world.

In order to be transformed into leather, salmon skins must be tanned and finished—a process that takes up to seven weeks. The skins are soaked, churned, fleshed, and dried to remove scales, oils, and remnants of meat. Traditional tanning employs acid and lime, toxic materials that must be disposed of in the environment. The chemicals used to process salmon leather, however, are less toxic than those for processing mammal hides because fish scales are easier to remove from the skin than hair.

Salmon leather's natural color is a beautiful, creamy white. The pelts can then be soaked in vegetable dye to take on a variety of deep, bright colors and a glossy finish. Chrome dyeing (a more toxic process) yields softer colors and a suede-like surface. The dyed skins are dried and then softened with oils to yield a thin, flexible, resilient material whose strength is greater than that of most land leathers. What is more, fish leather does not smell like fish.

Salmon is essential to the local economy in many parts of Alaska, where commercial fisheries are the state's largest employer. The Nature Conservancy is working with its partners to restore key fish habitats and slow the effects of climate change. If conducted in an ecologically and socially sound manner, the manufacture of salmon leather has the potential to further enrich the economy by turning waste into a renewable source of valuable material.

isaac mizrahi

ISAAC MIZRAHI

ISAAC MIZRAHI

An outspoken voice on the American fashion scene, Isaac Mizrahi is an icon, celebrity, performer, and talented designer of women's and men's wear. Born and raised in Brooklyn, New York, he started designing clothes when he was thirteen, and he launched his first fashion line at fifteen. Since then, he has embarked on numerous adventures in art, business, and public life, with fashion lines ranging from high end to mass market.

Mizrahi is the subject of the documentary film *Unzipped*, has starred in his own TV show, and authored his own comic books. Mizrahi worked alongside fashion heroes like Calvin Klein, and helped the retail chain Target bring the concept of high design into everyday households. In 2008, he became creative director of Liz Claiborne, Inc., where he has the opportunity to wield enormous influence on popular taste as well as the means to explore sustainable practices in mass production.

A figure equipped with so much personal energy and public prominence is ideally suited to experiment with new materials for fashion. The Nature Conservancy commissioned Mizrahi to work with salmon skin. Mizrahi's design features leather paillettes—small disks akin to sequins that are sewn into a supporting layer of fabric to create a rich, fluid surface. Previous Mizrahi projects include cutting paillettes from aluminum soda cans, a cheeky experiment in using trash to create luxury.

For The Nature Conservancy, Mizrahi created a one-of-a-kind ensemble with matching shoes, an experience that exposed him to an exciting, new substance whose elegant appearance belies its humble origins. Such experiments could spark demand for a material that is poised to reduce waste and stimulate local economies.

New York fashion designer Isaac Mizrahi during a fitting session. Mizrahi used salmon leather to create an ensemble that includes a dress, jacket, and shoes.

Although salmon skin is often a waste product of the salmon industry, it can be salvaged and processed to make strong and durable leather. Captivated by the smooth,

To create a short dress and complementary long jacket, Mizrahi used a base fabric of silk chiffon that lightly skims the body. He then had the salmon leather paillettes

By using thousands of slightly overlapping paillettes in his dress and jacket, Mizrahi recalls the scales of a fish with his design and celebrates the animal's grace and

subtile texture of the salmon leather, Mizrahi sent the undyed leather to Paris to be cut into paillettes.

hand-sewn onto the fabric. Finally, he designed a pair of open-back, high-heeled shoes using salmon leather from undyed whole skins that he adorned with rhinestones.

beauty. Through this project, Mizrahi demonstrates how a product that is traditionally disposed of as trash can be transformed into a luxurious piece of fashion.

salmon leather commission

Isaac Mizrahi's salmon-leather ensemble consists of a short dress worn with a long jacket that trails on the floor like a mermaid tail. Mizrahi worked with a Parisian maker of fashion embellishments to turn pelts of salmon leather into paillettes. First, the leather was skived (shaved down to make it thinner), then die-cut it into small disks perforated for sewing.

Rather than use dyed leather, Mizrahi chose to work with the soft ivory color that results from the basic processing of discarded fish skins into finished leather. Sewn by hand onto a base fabric, the paillettes create an undulating, irregular surface that reflects light and dramatizes the inherent motion of the garment as it is worn—not unlike the scales of a fish. Open-back shoes, also made from salmon leather, complete the look. Reflecting back on the process, Mizrahi comments, "Who knew that salmon skin could be so resilient? I always think of salmon skin as something you peel off your food, but in fact, it is a beautiful substance."

Mizrahi's sketches show the lean, simple profile of his salmon-leather jacket and dress.

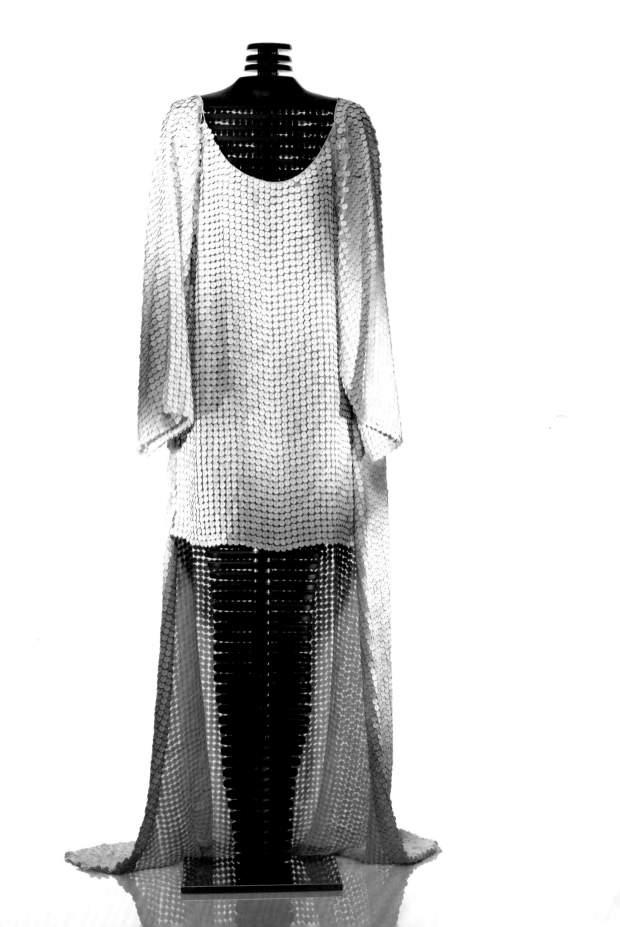

"Design is the most personal thing in the world,
but at the same time, it's not personal at all.
My approach in this project was to give equal weight
to ecology and glamour." *Isaac Mizrahi*

SPECIFICATIONS

Dimensions (H X W X D):
page 127: dress: 86.4 X
48.3 CM (34 X 19 IN.)
robe: 170.2 X 53.3CM
(5 FT. 7 IN. X 21 X IN.)

page 130: 12.1 X 21.6 X 10.2
CM (4 3/4 X 8 1/2 X 4 IN.)

Materials: calf leather
(shoe), organza,
rhinestones, salmon skin

SOURCING

The salmon leather used
in the commission was
purchased from Fine Exotic
Leather, which prepares
salmon skin from Alaska and
Canada. The paillettes were
prepared by Langlois-Martin
in Paris.

SUPPORT

Object photography
on pages 127–30
by Jay Zukerkorn.

maya forest, mexico

TOP Children play music inside their family's cooking hut. About 130 families live in Veinte de Noviembre.

BOTTOM LEFT *Chiclero* Elias Cahuich stands near his ponies outside his home in Veinte de Noviembre.

BOTTOM RIGHT Children from Veinte de Noviembre, an ejido named after the day it was founded in 1971.

PREVIOUS PAGE View from an ancient Mayan temple. Thousands of Mayan structures have been identified within the Calakmul Biosphere Reserve, 90% of which remain unexplored. The great Mayan City of Calakmul lies at the heart of the Reserve in the state of Campeche.

Dense, lush, and brimming with life, the Maya Forest forms the heart of Mexico's Yucatán Peninsula and is the lifeblood of the small *ejido*, or village, Veinte de Noviembre.

Here, the sounds of children calling to each other in Yucatec Maya mix with the cries of white-fronted parrots and howler monkeys. Fantastically colored toucans, motmots, oropendolas, and manakins fly in and out of the forest canopy. Giant palm fans, orchids, and bromeliads form the backdrop for anteaters, agoutis, tapirs, and tamaduas. The jaguars, pumas, and ocelots that prowl the forest floor are part of the most significant cat population in North America. This remarkable array of plant and animal life is matched only by the mystery of Mayan ruins scattered throughout the forest—remnants of an ancient and magnificent past.

Pieces of this past live on in forestry ejidos like Veinte de Noviembre, where some 130 families live and work. Inside one-room thatched wooden homes, women weave hammocks, embroider *huipil*, a traditional Mayan dress, or tend the family garden outside. Nearby, men look after beehives or work in the forest harvesting trees or extracting chicle from the *chicozapote* tree. Many ejidos were formed solely for the purpose of extracting chicle, and for nearly seventy years, chicle harvesting has provided steady income to local people.

Today, road construction, tourism development, agricultural expansion, land speculation, and forest fires are altering the Maya Forest and threatening the food, water, medicine, and livelihoods the forest provides to surrounding communities. In Mexico, many local people are abandoning the forest for better economic opportunities elsewhere, leaving it vulnerable to exploitation.

Ejidos like Veinte de Noviembre provide a way to preserve income, culture, and biological diversity; most forestry ejidos maintain more than 90 percent of their lands as tropical forest. The Nature Conservancy is working with ejidos and local communities to improve the management of natural resources, implement sustainable—and more profitable—forestry practices, develop ecotourism opportunities, and control and prevent forest fires. This combination of strong conservation science with indigenous traditions provides the best hope for the future of Mexico's Maya Forest.

chicle latex

TOP Chicle is melted at a temperature of about 115 degrees centigrade until it resembles thick maple syrup and poured into molds, where it hardens into blocks to be sold to gum dealers.

BOTTOM LEFT A *chiclero* cuts the bark of a *Manilkara zapota* tree in a zig-zag pattern to reach the sap. The process does not harm the tree.

BOTTOM RIGHT Chicle flows from a tree after it has been tapped.

Of all the materials explored in this exhibition, chicle may be the most unorthodox as a design material. This substance commands a long history of sustainable stewardship. Chicle latex flows from the *Manilkara zapota*, a tree that grows in the rainforest of Belize, Guatemala, Mexico, and Nicaragua. Unlike other latex-producing trees, the *M. zapota* has never been successfully cultivated in plantations. Thus, chicle harvesting has always taken place within the forest. For thousands of years, the Mayan people have chewed on chicle, enjoying its naturally sweet taste and sticky texture. During the zenith of the Aztec civilization, prostitutes attracted customers by snapping their chicle as they chewed it.

The dream of converting chicle into rubber fueled the "discovery" of this material by Western industry. In 1867, the exiled Mexican leader Antonio López de Santa Anna approached Thomas Addams, an inventor in New York City, with the hopes of vulcanizing chicle to yield a stable material. When Addams failed, he was left with nearly two tons of chicle in his lab. Remembering from Santa Anna that chicle was popular for chewing, Addams tried his hand at making gum, which in the United States at the time consisted of sweetened paraffin wax. He thus invented modern chewing gum (as well as machines for dispensing gum balls to the public).

An industry was born, and several North American manufacturers dominated the chicle business for decades to come, paying the local *chicleros* low wages to harvest the material in the forest and process it into blocks of raw material for export. After synthetic gum base was invented in 1944–45, the market for chicle rapidly declined. Today, small amounts of natural chicle are still used in gum, and there is a growing interest in organic, natural variants of the product, as well as in the health benefits of chewing gum. Chicle is a nontimber forest product that can be sustainably harvested while boosting local economies. Because the *M. zapota* tree grows in the forest, protecting these trees also helps protect the surrounding ecosystem.

hella jongerius

PUSHED WASHTUB, 1996
Sink

NON-TEMPORARY, 2005
Vase

THE WORKER, 2006
Chair

Dutch designer Hella Jongerius stretches chicle latex in her studio in Rotterdam as she experiments with the material's practical uses.

Hella Jongerius, known for her unusual use of materials and her interest in mixing craft processes with advanced industrial techniques, is among the world's leading experimental designers. Based in Rotterdam, Jongerius has been creating influential designs for textiles, furniture, vessels, and other objects since the early 1990s. She is a leading voice within the distinctive design community of the Netherlands, stimulating a global discourse on materials, functionality, and production. Her studio, Jongeriuslab, creates short-run, one-of-a-kind experimental works as well as objects for mass production.

Jongerius often combines diverse elements and techniques to create overtly collaged products, such as ceramic vases with stitching and perforation, as well as sofas upholstered in shifting colors of wool. Her Long Neck and Groove vases combine parts cut from existing vessels and bound together with tape. Jongerius's Pushed Soft Washtub, a bathroom fixture made from flexible polyurethane, places a resilient material into a domestic space where cold, hard surfaces are expected.

Conservation functions as both medium and metaphor across Jongerius's work, as she has sought to reuse abandoned materials as well as recombine existing textile patterns or bring new energy to traditional craft practices. In place of the seamless sameness favored by mass production, she seeks out variation, imperfection, and change. Many pieces suggest a process of coming undone as much as a process of completion.

The Nature Conservancy partnered with Jongerius to explore the potential of chicle latex, a substance never before used in product design. She approached this daunting task with the open mind of a scientist and explorer, investigating its adhesive properties and molding characteristics. As a complement to Jongerius's chicle project, Glee Gum—one of today's leading makers of organic, chicle-based chewing gum, based in Providence, Rhode Island—is creating a *Design for a Living World* gum flavored with cardamom and honey from the Yucatán.

In its raw state, chicle latex is a milky-white liquid. To transform it into a usable material, the chicleros of the ejido Veinte de Noviembre heat it in a large pot over an

When the dried bricks of chicle latex arrived at Hella Jongerius's studio in the Netherlands, she began exploring the design potential of a product largely associated with

Jongerius discovered that chicle heated at lower temperatures yielded a viscous substance that made an excellent adhesive and could be wound around object

open flame until it reaches a thick, elastic, almost rubbery consistency. It is then poured into molds and allowed to dry into bricks for easy shipping.

hewing gum. She experimented with the material by melting it back to a liquid at different temperatures and pulling and stretching it into thin strips to test its elasticity.

bind them together. Chicle heated at higher temperatures resulted in a thin, dark-brown liquid that she applied to ceramic surfaces as a decorative element.

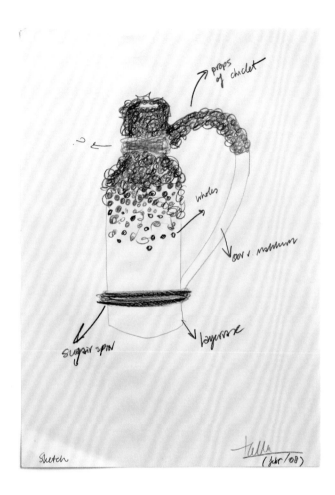

Sketch

chicle collection

Jongeriuslab is a design studio that experiments with diverse forms and materials. It is at once a kitchen, workshop, and factory that buzzes with activity. Hella Jongerius traveled to the Maya Forest to observe the harvesting and preparation of natural chicle by members of Veinte de Noviembre. During her five-day trip through the rainforest, she observed the chicleros extracting latex from the trees and processing it into bricks for sale on the international market.

Back in her studio, Jongerius found chicle difficult to tame. The designer explored melting, molding, stretching, winding, and shaping the material into stable objects. In a series of large-scale ceramic vessels, she used chicle's elastic and adhesive properties to create rich tactile surfaces and planes of connection between diverse materials.

In her designs, Jongerius used chicle latex as decoration, an adhesive, and a bind. Her sketch above demonstrates all three of these applications.

"The chicle was hard to understand. I was working like an alchemist trying to find a better function than chewing on it." *Hella Jongerius*

SPECIFICATIONS

Dimensions (H X W X D):
page 143, left: 29.8 X 24.1 X 14 CM (11 3/4 X 9 1/2 X 5 1/2 IN.)

page 143, right: 19.1 X 17.8 X 7.6 CM (7 1/2 X 7 X 3 IN.)

page 144, left: 49.5 X 12.7 CM (19 1/2 X 5 IN.)

page 144, right: 51.4 X 11.4 CM (20 1/4 X 4 1/2 IN.)

page 145: 40.6 X 21.6 CM (16 X 8 1/2 IN.)

page 146: 73.7 X 40.6 X 22.9 CM (29 X 16 X 9 IN.)

Materials: chicle, glass, plastic, porcelain

SOURCING

Samples of chicle latex were provided by Verve, Inc., makers of Glee Gum. Chicle was also purchased from the chicleros in the Veinte de Noviembre ejido. Ceramics designed by Hella Jongerius provide the base for the chicle experiments.

SUPPORT

Special thanks to the members of the Veinte de Noviembre ejido, Deborah Shimberg at Verve Inc., Emerald Planet, and Tropicarural Americana.

Object photography on pages 142–46 by Dan Whipps.

idaho

lava lake ranch, idaho

TOP A field of blue penstemon, a flower indigenous to Idaho that can survive periods of severe drought.

BOTTOM Two shepherds herd sheep on the Lava Lake Ranch.

PREVIOUS PAGE Sheep from the Lava Lake Ranch are herded through the town of Hailey, Idaho, as they make their way to high-mountain grazing grounds for the summer.

Like the herds of elk and mule deer that migrate from valley to high country, the sheep of Lava Lake Ranch in Hailey, Idaho, travel hundreds of miles every summer. During the day, they dine on native grasses, forbs, and wildflowers as herders on horseback guide them to higher pasture. As night falls on the herders' camp above the Snake River Plain, border collies and Great Pyrenees dogs keep watch for wolves, coyotes, and other predators.

The view from here has changed little since settlers rolled through in covered wagons. Rugged mountains give way to wild, unbroken stretches of land alive with pronghorn antelope, bears, and mountain goats. The lone white top of a sheep wagon—the self-contained, portable home of a sheepherder—is the only structure for miles.

Sheep ranching has been a cornerstone of local economies since the late 1800s and continues here much as it has in the past. Today, thousands of acres of ranchland help preserve large mammal migrations by connecting public lands. But these open spaces are at risk from the kind of unplanned development occurring across the Rocky Mountains. As one of the fastest-growing states in the country, Idaho will increasingly have to balance the region's economic and environmental needs.

Lava Lake Ranch is forging a new path in sheep ranching— one that seeks to preserve the fabric of this large, unfragmented landscape while using the land thoughtfully and carefully. Committed to coexisting with even its wildest neighbors, Lava Lake manages predators with nonlethal techniques such as guard dogs and electrified fences, and devotes 100 percent of its profits to conservation. Working with The Nature Conservancy, the ranch maintains an active science and research program and has developed a plan to conserve the native ecosystem. The ranch has already permanently protected 7,500 acres with conservation easements. And because its sheep wander across nearly one million acres of public land, the ranch also works closely with state and federal wildlife agencies.

Ranchers have always had a deep connection to the land. With its exceptional commitment to conservation, Lava Lake Ranch offers a model for living off the land that respects the environment and preserves it for both people and wildlife.

organic wool

TOP The color of wool can vary depending on the type of sheep.

BOTTOM Lava Lake protects its sheep through nonlethal methods, including the use of Great Pyrenees guard dogs, which are extremely effective at repelling predators.

People have grazed sheep on open land for millennia, using these animals as a source of meat, milk, leather, and fibers. Sheep can sustain themselves on the natural landscape, while cattle and pigs are generally fed larger amounts of harvested grains. Sheep eat not only grass (preferred by cattle) but also woody materials, such as tree forage and shrubs, as well as herbaceous plants that other animals reject. By eagerly consuming invasive "forbs" such as leafy spurge, spotted knapweed, and tall larkspur, sheep help control non-native weeds that would otherwise be treated with herbicides.

Because of their diverse diets, sheep ultimately require less fossil fuel to raise than other animals, while also providing humans with wool fibers, a valuable, renewable material. Grazing sheep can be rotated with crops, making farmlands more productive. Although overgrazing damages the land, sustainable practices such as reseeding and brush control allow sheep farming to interact successfully with local ecologies. Agroforestry, a practice now implemented around the world, combines animal grazing with farming and the cultivation of new forests. By controlling weeds and leaving behind manure, sheep help young trees to survive and flourish.

Predators are a constant threat to sheep. On the rangelands of the American West, the wolf is joined by coyotes, mountain lions, bears, and other creatures that prey on lambs. Such predators find their home in The Nature Conservancy's Silver Creek Preserve, which lies adjacent to Lava Lake Ranch. The ranch uses Great Pyrenees dogs to repel predators without lethal force, assigning at least two dogs to each roving band of sheep. These beautiful and loyal work animals form deep bonds with the flocks they protect. The Panama sheep, which provided the wool for this project, graze solely on land that has not been treated with pesticides or other chemicals. The wool they produce is certified organic.

christien meindertsma

POUFS, 2008
Seating

FLOCKS, 2007
Mittens

Although wool is warm, tactile, and rooted in nature, most people do not stop to think about where it comes from. Christien Meindertsma takes her materials personally, celebrating their points of origin in the natural world. In her internationally acclaimed Flocks project, this young graduate of the Design Academy Eindhoven in the Netherlands works with farmers to build one-on-one relationships with the living sheep and rabbits that provide materials for her work. Each of her pieces—whether a sweater, pair of gloves, or furniture element—is made from fibers collected from a single animal. A graphic identity card for each creature accompanies her products, inviting users to recognize the real, living animals that supply comfort and beauty to human beings.

To make her rugs and poufs, Meindertsma uses a felting process to create skeins of unusually thick yarn. She employs oversized knitting needles to generate familiar knitted patterns at a dramatically enlarged scale. Meindertsma contributes fresh ideas to the widespread revival of craft that has inspired countless designers, artists, and citizens around the world to reconnect with hand processes. By definition, all craft work actively engages materials, techniques, and a rhythmic sense of time stretched across an act of creation. Meindertsma redoubles that effect by harvesting her own materials and making her own tools.

The Nature Conservancy paired Meindertsma with lambs and sheep at the Lava Lake Ranch in Idaho. The animals provided wool for a large rug composed of modular parts; each one is made from 3 1/2 pounds of wool, equal to the yield of a single sheep. These animals—and the regional landscape in which they thrive— bring life to the textiles she creates.

Dutch designer Christien Meindertsma accompanies a flock of sheep as it moves through Hailey, Idaho, to greener pastures. Meindertsma worked closely with Lava Lake's owners to learn more about the animals that provided the wool for her project.

This felted, double-stranded yarn was made from wool provided by the sheep of Lava Lake Ranch. Meindertsma was surprised to find that the organic wool from Lava

She knitted a series of hexagonal wool tiles using a variety of common patterns. To knit with such thick wool, she employs knitting needles the size of yardsticks.

Meindertsma chose the shape of a hexagon for each tile to suggest the abstract profile of a sheep—with four feet, a head, and a tail. Knitted together, these "sheep"

Lake is softer than the wool she normally uses. She works with extra thick yarn that highlights her knitting technique as well as emphasizes the beauty of the material.

The tiles hook together with 4-by-6-inch frog-like clasps. To shape the clasps, she cut open the wool, slipped a wire through it, and bent it into the correct figure.

create a flock. Because the rug is comprised of individual 30-by-27-inch tiles, it can be reconfigured in multiple ways and tailored to a particular room's size and shape.

wool commission

Christien Meindertsma's hand-knitted carpet is crafted from hexagonal modules that are hooked together into a larger "flock" with frog-like clasps. The organic wool was provided by Panama sheep from Lava Lake Ranch. Each module uses 3 1/2 pounds of fiber, the amount yielded by a single sheep.

Meindertsma makes her own felted wool and knits it together with oversize needles. By rendering traditional sweater stitches at a large scale, Meindertsma casts familiar textures in a new light, drawing attention to the material by amplifying its presence. Identity cards, or "passports," link samples of each material with portraits of the flock.

Each of the eleven tiles in Meindertsma's rug represents the yield of a single sheep.

"A lot of the value of a product lies in knowing where it comes from, how it grows, and in what amounts. This information tends to get lost when things are made all around the world and not in your own backyard." *Christien Meindertsma*

SPECIFICATIONS

Dimensions (H X W X D):
pages 159–62:
11 tiles each measuring
76.2 X 69.9 X 10.2 CM
(30 X 27 1/2 X 4 IN.)

Materials: wire, wool

SOURCING

The wool for the flock rug comes from Lava Lake Ranch's organic band of Panama sheep that roam the hills of southern Idaho, covering almost one hundred miles during their yearly journey. The wool, extremely dirty when shorn, was washed and prepared by Thirteen Mile Lamb and Wool Company, which also sells organic yarn. It was then sent to the Netherlands, where it was spun and knit into the rug tiles.

SUPPORT

Special thanks to Kathleen Bean, Mike Stevens, and Cheryl Bennett at Lava Lake Ranch, and John Plummer from Cinema Story Entertainment, LLC.

Object photography on pages 159–62 by Roel van Tour.

china

yunnan province, china

TOP Tibetan Buddhist prayer flags hang over a valley in the mountainous Yunnan Province.

BOTTOM LEFT A Tibetan woman walks up the stairs in her home, where elders hold a monthly Buddhist prayer ceremony.

BOTTOM RIGHT A farmer stops water in an irrigation canal. Yunnan's rivers — the Yangtze, Irrawaddy, Salween, and Mekong — supply approximately one in ten people on Earth with food, water, transportation, and trade.

PREVIOUS PAGE The flagstone pavements of the Old Town area of Lijiang, China, are lined with wooden, tile-roofed courtyard houses. Lijiang is located between Yunnan province and Tibet.

Four of Asia's great rivers course through China's Yunnan Province, carving out deep gorges at the base of steep, jagged mountains. Smaller streams traverse primeval-looking forests of bamboo and pine, where Asiatic black bears, red pandas, and Yunnan golden monkeys roam. A nearly perpetual fog hangs over trees that drip with mosses and lichens. Up and down these mountains are the homes and terraced farm fields of the region's fifteen ethnic groups.

In the village of Zhuyuan, in southern Yunnan, the sharp smell of fiery chilies drifts through open courtyards, in which men and women sit fashioning stools, vases, and a variety of baskets from bamboo. Integral to families' livelihoods for centuries, bamboo is now cultivated in small plots around the village. Other villagers gather to dry tobacco leaves on tall towers just outside the town. Across the village, past rice, corn, and tobacco fields, red soil colors the waters of the Yangtze River.

Today, deforestation and forest degradation caused by development and growing energy needs are affecting Yunnan's spectacular biological diversity. Fuel-wood collection alone accounts for the loss of thousands of acres of forest every year. Poaching threatens wildlife, especially the endangered Yunnan golden monkey, which survives in isolated populations.

Sustainable economic-development efforts like bamboo harvesting and ecotourism preserve Yunnan's diverse natural resources, supply communities with income, and help restore the balance between people and nature. To reduce wood consumption, The Nature Conservancy is introducing bio-gas furnaces, solar panels, and fuel-efficient stoves into homes, schools, and monasteries. Working with Chinese partners, the Conservancy has installed more than 12,000 alternative-energy units in more than 400 villages across Yunnan Province.

The Conservancy is also working with the Chinese government to increase protection of Yunnan's natural areas by establishing a system of national parks. In 2007, it helped China create its first national park, Pudacuo National Park. By protecting some of Yunnan's most important ecological treasures and by providing jobs and resources for local communities, Pudacuo will be a model for China's new national-park system.

bamboo

TOP LEFT Bamboo is
a member of the
grass family and can
grow more than 50
meters high.

TOP RIGHT Yunnan's
forests of bamboo and
pine contain red pandas,
black-necked cranes,
and Yunnan golden
monkeys.

BOTTOM Zhang Ziming
was once a hunter and
now works with The
Nature Conservancy
to track and research
the endangered golden
monkey in the Laojun
Mountain area.

Some 600 million people around the globe rely on bamboo for their livelihoods. Although it can grow more than 50 meters high, this remarkable plant is not a tree, but a member of the grass family. It has an astonishing range of human uses—it is eaten as food, pulped into fibers for fabric, milled into strips to create flooring and veneer, and joined together in its unprocessed state as "vegetal steel" for constructing furniture and buildings. Bamboo is native to every continent on Earth except Antarctica and Europe. Used in combination with other materials and simple building techniques, bamboo can provide the basis of durable housing suitable for nearly any climate.

Bamboo has ecological as well as human benefits. It generates more oxygen than trees and absorbs large amounts of carbon. Requiring minimal water to flourish, bamboo helps purify the soil and the atmosphere. Bamboo forests provide habitats for various animal species. Capable of growing up to a meter in a single day, bamboo takes three years to mature, while an oak tree takes twenty. Because they shoot up from a system of roots, new stalks regenerate automatically after cutting, making replanting unnecessary.

With careful stewardship, bamboo is an ideal material for building. In 2008, the first FSC-certification (Forest Stewardship Council) for bamboo products was granted to Smith and Fong, a North American importer, paving the way for more certified bamboo products. As with any forest product, standards are critical. Bamboo harvested too early yields materials that are soft and easily damaged, and the exploding demand for bamboo provokes the clear-cutting of trees, allowing monoculture plantations to threaten biodiversity. Bamboo can invade nearby forests, crowding out other forms of vegetation. And breaking down bamboo into fibers for textiles can be a chemical-intensive process, while many bamboo flooring and veneer products are bound with toxic formaldehyde-based glues. Yet when these problems are addressed effectively, bamboo can become one of the world's most ecofriendly materials.

ezri tarazi

DEFOCUS
Metal and vinyl armchair

YESTERDAY'S
NEWSPAPERS, 2002
Paper armchair

NEW BAGHDAD, 2005
Aluminum table

Israeli industrial and
furniture designer Ezri
Tarazi explores the
structural properties of
bamboo in his studio.
His installation of
bamboo totems moves
the dense landscape
of China's bamboo
forests indoors, creating
a domestic forest that
supports a range of
living arrangements.

"Green design" is a matter of course in Israel, a country endowed with limited resources and abundant ingenuity. Ezri Tarazi is a leading voice in Israel's vibrant design scene, where his work as a designer, teacher, curator, and critic has brought international attention to the country's design culture. Like many designers in Israel, Tarazi collaborates with partners around the globe; he works with equal ease on one-of-a-kind studio experiments and on high-technology products for worldwide distribution.

Conservation and the reuse of materials are ongoing concerns in Tarazi's work. To create a chair called Yesterday's Newspapers, he rolled up papers and bound them together with a rubber strap. To make seats and backs for his Defocus armchairs, he recycled roadside banners printed in Hebrew and Arabic. On a larger and potentially more influential scale, Tarazi has joined a global team of scientists, engineers, and investors to found Zenith Solar. The company created a new technology that uses mirrors and lenses to concentrate the sun's rays, yielding a system five times more efficient than traditional photovoltaic cells and far more economical to manufacture. Careful design planning is crucial to the product's success. Zenith's 10-square-meter dish is made from recycled plastic (manufactured with one of the world's largest injection molds) and is fitted with inexpensive mirrors attached with simple clips, allowing for easy maintenance.

An intense engagement with materials characterizes Tarazi's work at every level. For his New Baghdad table, manufactured by the Italian furniture maker Edra, he sliced lengths of extruded aluminum—a commonplace industrial material—into short sections, which he then assembled to make a perforated tabletop resembling a map of the city of Baghdad.

When the Conservancy commissioned Tarazi to experiment with bamboo, he chose to use the material as a structure rather than a surface. The result is a family of totemlike objects that use the plant's open core to support a variety of functions in the home, from media and audio to bookshelves and lighting.

Once the bamboo reached Israel from China, it spent more than a month tied up in customs. A total of 40 stalks were shipped, each averaging about 8–9 feet in

Bamboo is a hollow grass that can be easily cut into rings. Tarazi later used the rings to create a chair. Overall, he found the material to be surprisingly challenging to work

Tarazi cut holes and other openings into the stalks. By incorporating items such as speakers, lights, and shelves into the bamboo, he created unique, functiona

height. Designers at Tarazi Studio experimented extensively with the bamboo. They had been expecting thinner stalks, but the thick material raised many possibilities.

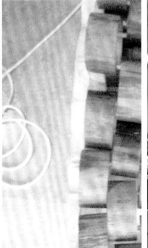

with—it was difficult to polish, was covered in scratches, and varied in color from green to yellow to brown. When tested for strength, about half of the material cracked.

domestic items that efficiently utilize vertical and horizontal space. These objects retain the natural form and height of the natural organism without over-processing it.

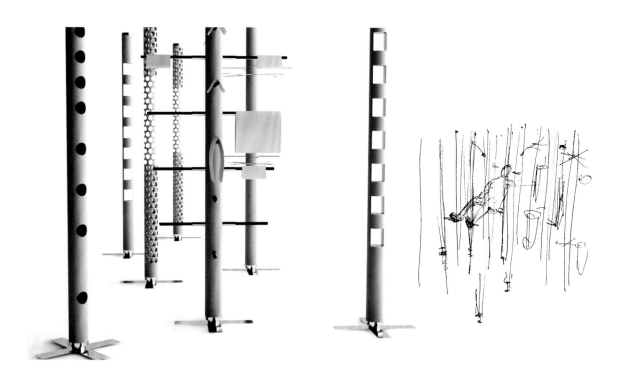

bamboo commission

Ezri Tarazi's Living Forest is made from thick stalks of bamboo
that cluster in the room like a grove of living grasses. The hollow
stalks have been cut and punctured to accommodate audio
speakers, wiring, lighting fixtures, and more. Tarazi avoided the
familiar technique of lashing together lengths of bamboo into
larger structures—an idiom seen in everything from makeshift
scaffolding to upscale decorative objects. Instead, he chose to
design precise, sophisticated connections and components using
metal and other materials while allowing the bamboo stalks
to keep their inherent dents and bruises.

   In one object, sleek table-tennis balls emerge from holes
drilled through a bamboo stem, and compact fluorescent lamps
installed inside allow these translucent balls to transmit light.
In a second piece resembling a giant flute, audio speakers peer
out through a series of punched holes. Another stalk has been
pierced with metal bars to create an ingenious magazine rack that
supports publications from their inner spines. A "media center"
holds an iMac, iPod, keyboard, and mouse. "Rather than use the
material as a surface," explains Tarazi, "our project enhances
the material to become an object in itself."

Tarazi's designs were
inspired by China's
natural environment.
Through his totems,
he sought to create a
functional system while
bringing a sense of a
bamboo forest into
living space.

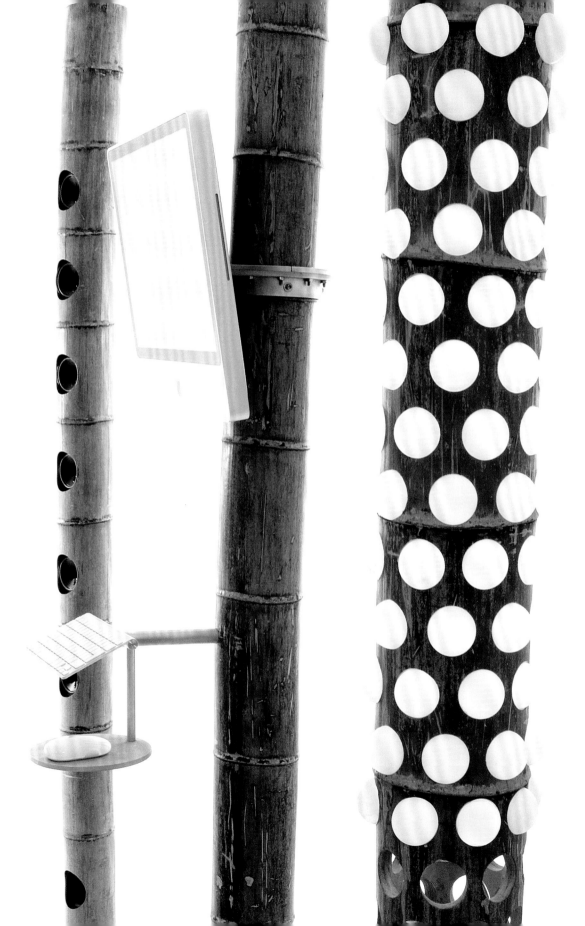

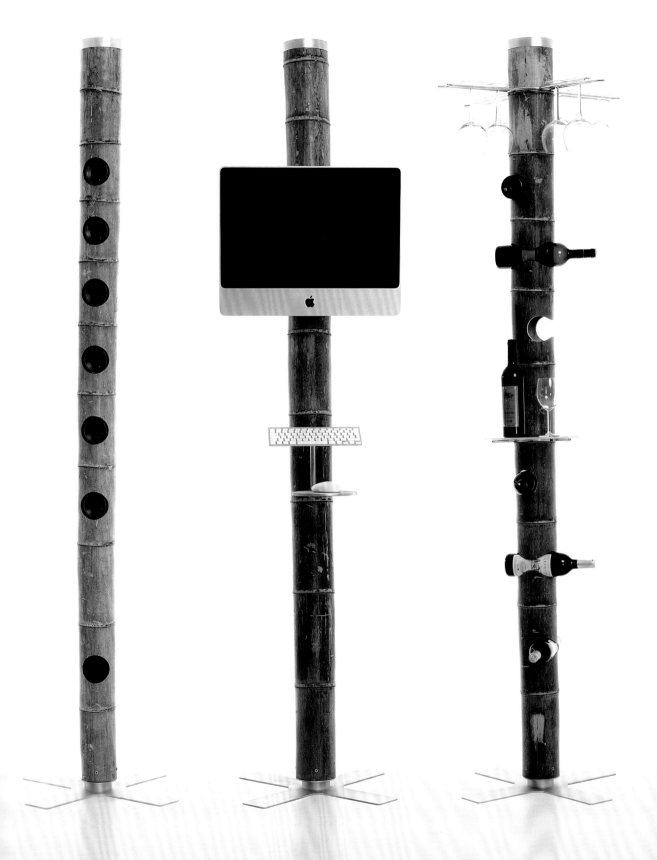

"The idea was to create the sense of a bamboo forest inside your living room, but instead of using the material as a decoration, which I see some people do, we gave all the pieces a function. My mission was to make a design object that is desirable and that doesn't take out the bamboo character." *Ezri Tarazi*

SPECIFICATIONS

Dimensions (H X W X D):
pages 175–77: 231.14 X 14.6 CM (91 X 5.75 IN.)

page 178: 71.1 X 51.4 X 153.7 CM (28 X 20.25 X 60.5 IN.)

Materials: bamboo, iMac, metal, ping-pong balls, plastic, speakers

SOURCING

The bamboo poles used in this commission were sourced from Anji Zhoumao Bamboo and Wood Industry Company in China, located through the International Network for Bamboo and Rattan (INBAR). INBAR is an international organization dedicated to improving the social, economic, and environmental benefits of bamboo and rattan that manages a database on bamboo and rattan trade on its Web site. The prototypes were made in Ezri Tarazi's studio, in collaboration with Roni Naim Ltd. and The Industrial Design Department Workshops, Bezalel Academy of Art and Design, Jerusalem.

SUPPORT

Special thanks to Apple Computers; Yoav Avinoam, Itay Amir, Maayan Hagar, Gil Shefi, and Yasmin Yotam from Tarazi Studio; and Michal Ronen-Tarazi.

Object photography on pages 174–78 provided courtesy of Tarazi Design Studio.

upper st. john river, maine

As winter moves into northern Maine, a heavy snow falls across the forest of the Upper St. John River. In this isolated landscape, a group of French-Canadian men and women, leaving their families behind and braving subzero temperatures, cross the border to carve out a living during the region's frozen logging season.

Using sustainable forestry practices and modern technology, they continue the area's long tradition of logging—one that goes back to the earliest French-Acadian settlers who used the Upper St. John River to drive logs downriver in the 1700s. Each day, the workers are out by 5:15 a.m., their trucks' headlights casting an eerie glow on a snow-covered forest of red maple, birch, cedar, and spruce—home to Canada lynx, moose, and black bear.

Every spring, the river groans and creaks as massive slabs of ice melt and break away. These ice chunks scour the banks and sweep away trees, leaving tumbled rocks for shoreline. Only the hardiest plants—such as St. John oxytrope and alpine sweet-broom—survive in such harsh circumstances.

These rough conditions and the region's remote location have kept it relatively pristine, yet threats exist. Fragmentation of habitat and ownership divides land into smaller and smaller parcels, making it difficult to protect large, intact landscapes. The region is also vulnerable to unsustainable forestry practices that jeopardize St. John's forest, watershed, and wildlife. Climate change is exacerbating these threats with disturbances in long-established seasonal patterns.

In the 1990s, The Nature Conservancy bought 286 square miles of forest around the Upper St. John River. While much of the forest is set aside as an ecological reserve, logging continues to be a critical part of the local economy. In an effort to preserve the landscape and provide jobs, the surrounding Conservancy lands have been certified under the sustainable-forestry guidelines of the Forest Stewardship Council, ensuring that all wood harvesting is carried out in an environmentally sound and socially beneficial manner. Protected areas within this working forest are expected to help plants and animals adapt to the effects of climate change.

As the logging season ends and the last trucks cross the flat, white landscape, the forest reverts to silence. The cycle of renewal for the land and people begins once more.

fsc-certified red maple

The Forest Stewardship Council certifies sustainable forest materials harvested around the world. Headquartered in Germany, the council provides conservationists, communities, businesses, and consumers with a means of assuring that wood, paper, and other forest-based products are harvested in a sustainable manner. FSC certification is market-based and nonregulatory—it is applied voluntarily, not imposed by law. It tracks a given material along its "chain of custody," following the path a raw material takes from its origins in the forest to its processing, export, import, and transformation into useful goods.

Designers are key consumers of forest products. By specifying materials used to make buildings, interiors, and consumer goods, they can affect the pulse of ecosystems elsewhere in the world. People walking into a room have no way of understanding where the surrounding surfaces and structures come from; for designers, however, this understanding becomes transparent through FSC.

Before awarding certification, the FSC performs independent, third-party audits of a forest's management. All FSC-certified forests must balance the economic use of working forests with the stewardship of biological diversity. Protecting the forest also preserves its long-term economic value. In more than eighty-two countries around the world, more than 220 million acres of forest operations have been certified by the FSC. Along the Upper St. John River, The Nature Conservancy owns 180,000 acres of land managed under FSC guidelines. Products bearing the FSC seal include those made from wood grown in part or in whole in certified forests. Goods made entirely from reclaimed and recycled materials can also be FSC-certified.

Although the FSC's programs have made strong and steady progress, the vast majority of the world's forests is harvested—and often plundered—without any ecological oversight. As designers and consumers demand that the goods and materials they purchase bear the FSC seal, pressure will rise to protect more forests for future life and use.

maya lin

2X4 LANDSCAPE, 2007
Systematic Landscapes

WATER LINE, 2007
Systematic Landscapes

ALTERED ATLAS, 2007
Systematic Landscapes

Maya Lin consistently explores how human constructions meet the earth. As an architecture student at Yale University, Lin stunned the world in 1981 by winning a national competition to design the Vietnam Veterans Memorial in Washington, D.C. By creating an object that sinks into the land rather than towering above it, she introduced a radically new model for monument design. Etched into the memorial's black granite surface are the names of 58,000 Americans who died or disappeared while fighting the war. With its low horizon and V shape, the Vietnam Veterans Memorial invites people to come in close and experience history and loss in an existential—rather than symbolic—way. While many veterans angrily opposed the design as a "black gash" in the landscape, the memorial quickly became a beloved pilgrimage site, receiving thousands of visitors each day.

Since then, Lin has continued to explore the undulations of the earth as an inspiration for the design of furniture, landscapes, installations, and memorials. Her project Groundswell, an installation inside the Wexner Center at Ohio State University, consists of glittering mounds of shattered automobile glass. Her Wave Field at the University of Michigan College of Engineering is a grass-covered soil structure whose complex topography mirrors the movement of waves through water. The curving roofline of her Weber Residence at Williams College in Williamstown, Massachusetts, echoes the mountains that engulf the campus.

Lin has tried her hand at furniture as well. Her Stones series, created for the modern-furniture manufacturer Knoll, consists of stools and tables made from single pieces of molded polypropylene. Her Longitude chaise, also designed for Knoll, offers up a subtly undulating seating plane.

Using FSC-certified hardwoods harvested from a working forest in Maine, Lin produced the Terra bench, a striking piece of furniture that highlights the beauty of an individual tree.

Architect, artist, and furniture designer Maya Lin in her studio in New York examines different types of FSC-certified wood from the St. John forest in northern Maine.

The wood used in Maya Lin's bench came from a single tree that was cut from a sustainably managed, FSC-certified forest on Nature Conservancy property in upper

The different layers of color in the wood reminded Lin of the layers of the earth. She decided to design a bench that echoed the topography of the forest surrounding th

Lin then stripped off the bark to reveal the inner properties of the wood, and kept the rounded edge of the trunk raw to recall the uneven terrain of the wood's origi

Maine. Lin chose to work with red maple because she was intrigued by the wood's perceived imperfections, including the variations of color throughout the lumber.

Upper St. John River. To create the effect, Lin cut the log of red maple into twenty individual planks measuring 48 inches long.

The planks were glued together (laminated) to create the bench's uneven surface, and four sturdy legs were attached.

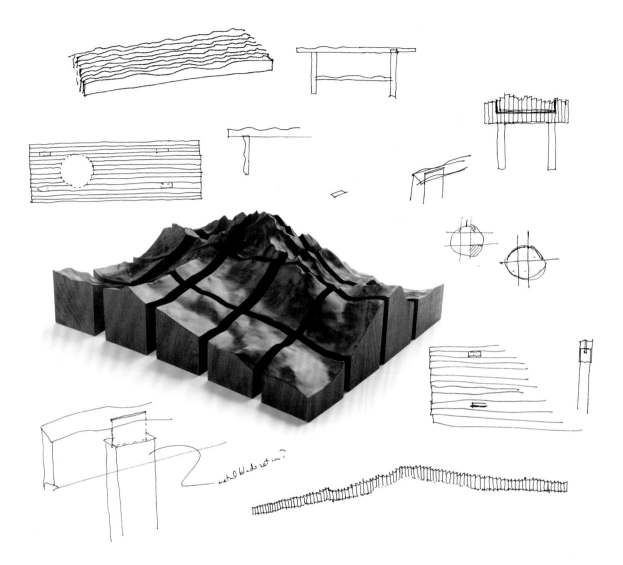

fsc-certified red maple commission

Maya Lin's Terra bench presents an unusual kind of surface. Rather than use milled lumber or flat sheet goods to make a plane, Lin pieced together lateral slices of timber to create an irregular, almost ragged plinth, allowing a broken, wave-like form to appear across the horizontal seating surface. Lin's project is a poetic rumination on how the vertical landscape of the forest is cut and aligned for use for chairs, tables, and other artifacts. Recalling Lin's large-scale topographical sculptures, the bench is both the fruit of the forest and a portrait of its terrain.

Lin's designs evoke the rugged terrain around the Upper St. John River in Maine.

"We tend to pollute that which we can't see. My work is about revealing the unseen in the natural world."
Maya Lin

SPECIFICATIONS

Dimensions (H X W X D):
pages 191–94:
38.1 X 121.9 X 51.1 CM
(15 X 48 X 20 1/8 IN.)

Materials: FSC-certified red maple, glue

SOURCING

The red maple used in the Terra bench was harvested, prepared, and shipped by Huber Resources Corporation, which works closely with The Nature Conservancy to manage the timber resources in the St. John forest. Custom milling and kiln drying was provided by Lumbra Hardwoods Inc. The bench was fabricated by Uhuru Design, a design-and-build furniture company dedicated to sustainability.

SUPPORT

Special thanks to Peter Triandafillou at Huber Resources Corporation and Bill Hilgandorf at Uhuru Design.

Object photography on pages 190–94 by Dan Whipps.

contributors

ANDY GRUNDBERG is a writer, curator, teacher, and arts consultant. He is currently the Associate Dean of Undergraduate Studies at the Corcoran College of Art and Design. From 1981–91, as a critic for the *New York Times*, he covered the rapid ascent of photography within the art world. Grundberg was director of The Friends of Photography in San Francisco (1992–97), and founded the quarterly journal *see*. Exhibitions organized include *Photography and Art: Interactions Since 1946* (1987) and *Points of Entry: Tracing Cultures* (1996). In 2001, he curated the exhibition *In Response to Place: Photographs from The Nature Conservancy's Last Great Places*, and developed the initial concept for *Design for a Living World* with The Nature Conservancy. Publications include *Crisis of the Real* (1999), *Mike and Doug Starn* (1990), and *Alexey Brodovitch* (1989). He has taught at Dartmouth College (Mellon Fellow, 1998–99), San Francisco Art Institute, School of Visual Arts, and University of Maryland.

ELLEN LUPTON is a writer, curator, and graphic designer. As curator of contemporary design at Cooper-Hewitt, National Design Museum, she has organized numerous exhibitions and publications, including *Mechanical Brides: Women and Machines from Home to Office* (1993), *Mixing Messages: Graphic Design and Contemporary Culture* (1996), *Letters from the Avant-Garde* (1996), *Skin: Surface, Substance + Design* (2002), and the *National Design Triennial* series (2000 to the present). She is director of the Graphic Design MFA program at Maryland Institute College of Art (MICA) in Baltimore, where she also serves as director of the Center for Design Thinking. At MICA she has produced a series of books with her students and colleagues, including *D.I.Y.: Design It Yourself* (2006), *Graphic Design: The New Basics* (with Jennifer Cole Phillips, 2008), *Indie Publishing: How to Design and Produce Your Own Book* (2008), and *Exploring Materials* (with Inna Alesina, forthcoming 2010).

ABBOTT MILLER is a designer, editor, art director, and curator whose body of work is founded on the relationship between design, writing, and photography. As editor and art director of the performing-arts journal *2wice*, he has collaborated with some of the world's most important choreographers and dancers. As a partner in the international design consultancy Pentagram, he has produced books, exhibitions, signage, Web sites, and identities for a wide range of clients, including Harley-Davidson, Whitney Museum of Art, the Guggenheim Museum, the Rock and Roll Hall of Fame, and the Freud Museum in Vienna. As an author and curator, he has explored design, art, architecture, and fashion though exhibitions and books. He has collaborated with artists and designers such as Matthew Barney, Yoko Ono, Nam-June Paik, Diller + Scofidio, and Merce Cunningham. He has curated and coauthored several exhibitions and books with Ellen Lupton, including *The Bathroom, the Kitchen, and the Aesthetics of Waste* (1992), *Design Writing Research* (1996), and *Swarm* (2006).

AMI VITALE is a photojournalist whose work has been recognized by World Press Photo, the NPPA, and International Photos of the Year. The South Asian Journalists Association presented her with the Daniel Pearl Award for outstanding print reporting on South Asia. Her stories have been awarded numerous grants and prizes, including the first-ever Inge Morath Grant by Magnum Photos, The Canon Female Photojournalist Award for her work in Kashmir, and an award from the Alexia Foundation for World Peace. Vitale's photographs have been published in magazines including *National Geographic, Adventure, Geo, Newsweek, Time, Smithsonian*, and *Le Figaro*. She has presented lectures for organizations around the world, and her images have been presented in international exhibitions including *Visa Pour L'Image*, (Perpignan, France), *Eyes on the World* (Istanbul, Turkey), *Reporters Sans Frontières* (Paris), the FotoArt Festival in Poland, and the Open Society Institute and The United Nations in New York. Now based in Washington, DC, Vitale is a contract photographer with *National Geographic* and frequently gives workshops throughout the Americas, Europe, and Asia.

tnc
acknowledgments

The Nature Conservancy wishes to thank the many people whose talent, time, and vision contributed to *Design for a Living World*.

First, a great deal of thanks is owed to Director Paul Warwick Thompson and the talented staff at Cooper-Hewitt. Their support made the book and the exhibition a reality.

Andy Grundberg, Holley Darden, and Jill Isenbarger first envisioned the project, inspired by the success of the *In Response to Place* photography exhibition. Andy's introductory essay skillfully connects the idea of interdisciplinary collaboration from *In Response to Place* to *Design for a Living World*. Jill Isenbarger guided the project from idea into reality. The project would not have been possible without her constant support.

Ellen Lupton and Abbott Miller were the creative force behind *Design for a Living World*, selecting the designers and editing the objects and images featured in the book and exhibition. They embraced the project, going above and beyond in a tireless pursuit of clarity, authenticity, and quality.

Ami Vitale traveled to ten locations in six months to capture the stunning images featured in the book and exhibition. Her dedication to her craft was an inspiration to everyone who had the great pleasure of working with her. The project was enhanced immeasurably by her participation.

Sara Elliott worked for two years to bring shape and substance to *Design for a Living World*, keeping an eye on the forest while minding the trees. Her contributions touch every aspect of the project. As a fierce advocate for the project and the Conservancy's mission, Emily Whitted met impossible deadlines with grace and style.

Gabrielle Antoniadas wrote the essays about each place, artfully creating the context for each commission. Ron Geatz and Martha Hodgkins contributed their keen editorial skills, helping to weave stories about design and conservation into a compelling whole.

Dozens of Nature Conservancy staff members contributed to making the commissions happen, from travel planning to translation to materials research. We would like to thank each and every one of them for their work on this project and for their dedication to protecting the lands and waters upon which all life depends. Special thanks are owed to Valerie Dorian, Amy Golden, M. Sanjayan, Sheri Turnbow, and Elizabeth Ward for their unwavering support of the project.

Kristen Spilman at Pentagram Design brought great sensitivity to the design of the book. Chul R. Kim, Director of Publications at Cooper-Hewitt, ensured that the book was both beautiful and as environmentally responsible as possible. Jeremy Hoffman and Brian Raby carried the same spirit into the design of the exhibition.

To the designers who rolled up their sleeves and contributed their time, talent, and compassion to the project, we are most grateful. Their engagement reminds us that the challenge of protecting the natural world requires creativity and innovation. The enthusiasm with which they participated makes us optimistic about the challenges we all face. For that we owe them a great deal of thanks.

The mission of The Nature Conservancy is to preserve the plants, animals and natural communities that represent the diversity of life on Earth by protecting the lands and waters they need to survive.

cooper-hewitt acknowledgments

Cooper-Hewitt, National Design Museum is grateful to the following individuals and organizations for their assistance and support during the preparation of the *Design for a Living World* exhibition and catalogue.

DESIGN TEAM
Museum Communications Design: Tsang Seymour Design: Patrick Seymour, Catarina Tsang, Andrew Hardy

Lighting Design: Jeffrey Nash Lighting Design

AT COOPER-HEWITT
Communications and Marketing: Jennifer Northrop, William Berry, Laurie Olivieri

Conservation: Lucy Commoner, Sarah Scaturro

Development and External Affairs: Caroline Baumann, Debbie Ahn, Sophia Amaro, Joanna Broughton, Deborah Fitzgerald, Kelly Gorman, Kelly Mullaney, Barbara Roan

Education: Caroline Payson, Shamus Adams, Mei Mah, Erin McCluskey, Alexander Tibbets

Exhibitions: Matthew O'Connor, Mathew Weaver

Finance: Christopher Jeannopoulos

Image Rights and Reproduction: Jill Bloomer

Operations: Diane Galt

Registrar: Steven Langehough, Melanie Fox, Larry Silver

design for a living world project credits

Editors: Ellen Lupton and Abbott Miller
TNC: Sara Elliott, Emily Whitted
Cooper-Hewitt: Chul R. Kim, Director of Publications
Book Design: Abbott Miller and Kristen Spilman, Pentagram
Exhibition Design: Abbott Miller, Jeremy Hoffman, Brian Raby, and Kristen Spilman, Pentagram
Principal Location Photography: Ami Vitale
Exhibition Fabrication: Design and Production Inc., Lorton, VA
Exhibition Graphic Production: Mega Media
Principal Videography: Ari Issler
Video Producer: Stella Cha
Video Editing: Toby Hayman
Special Thanks: Joan McCabe, Kurt Koepfle, Pentagram

photography

Principal photography by Ami Vitale: inside front cover, pages 1–10, 12, 14, 16, 18, 22, 24, 26, 28, 30, 35, 36–38, 40, 42, 44–45: TOP ROW: left, second from right; MIDDLE ROW: second from left, 46, 52–54, 68–70, 72, 84–86, 88, 100–102, 104, 108–109: TOP ROW: right; MIDDLE ROW: first three from left; ENTIRE BOTTOM ROW, 116–118, 120, 132–134, 136, 140–141: TOP ROW: first five from left, 148–150, 152: bottom, 154, 164–166, 168, 180–182, 184, inside back cover, back cover. **Timothy Hursley:** page 91: middle. **Philip Phorak:** page 91: top. **Brian Raby:** pages 44–45: TOP ROW: second and third from left, right; MIDDLE ROW: left, first three from right; ENTIRE BOTTOM ROW, 92–93: ENTIRE TOP ROW; MIDDLE ROW: first five images from left; BOTTOM ROW: first three images from left; right, 122, 124–125: TOP ROW: first five images from right; ENTIRE MIDDLE ROW, 188–189: TOP ROW: first three from right; ENTIRE BOTTOM ROW. **Mackenzie Stroh:** pages 58, 60–61: BOTTOM ROW: first four from left, 74, 90, 93: MIDDLE ROW: right; BOTTOM ROW: second from right, 106, 124–125: BOTTOM ROW, 170, 186. **Roel Van Tour:** pages 138, 140–41: ENTIRE MIDDLE ROW; ENTIRE BOTTOM ROW, 156–157: all images excluding top left, 159–162. **Dan Whipps:** pages 62–66, 77: bottom right, 78, 80–82, 110–114, 124: top left, 126, 142–146, 152: top left and right, 156: top left, 158, 188: top left, 190–194. **Jay Zukerkorn:** front cover, pages 47–50, 79, 95–98, 127–130. **Images provided courtesy of the artist:** pages 43, 59, 60–61: ENTIRE TOP ROW; ENTIRE MIDDLE ROW; BOTTOM ROW: last two images from left, 75, 76–77: ENTIRE TOP ROW; ENTIRE MIDDLE ROW; BOTTOM ROW: first four images from left, 94, 107, 108–109: TOP ROW: first four images from left; MIDDLE ROW: first two images from right, 123, 139, 141: top right, 155, 171–178, 188–189: top row: first four images from right; MIDDLE ROW: left, 187.

Design for a Living World
Edited by Ellen Lupton and Abbott Miller
© 2009 The Nature Conservancy
4245 North Fairfax Drive
Arlington, VA 22203
www.nature.org

Published by
Cooper-Hewitt, National Design Museum
Smithsonian Institution
2 East 91st Street
New York, NY 10128
www.cooperhewitt.org

Published on the occasion of the exhibition
Design for a Living World
Design inspired by The Nature Conservancy's Campaign
for a Sustainable Planet
at Cooper-Hewitt, National Design Museum,
Smithsonian Institution,
May 14, 2009–January 4, 2010.

design for a living world

is organized by

The Nature Conservancy
Protecting nature. Preserving life.

The exhibition's presentation at Cooper-Hewitt is made
possible in part by Enid and Lester Morse.

Additional support is provided by Esme Usdan.

This publication is made possible in part by
The Andrew W. Mellon Foundation.

Distributed to the trade in North America by
Assouline Publishing
601 West 26th Street, 18th floor
New York, NY 10001
www.assoulineusa.com

First edition: May 2009
ISBN: 978-0-910503-88-4
Library of Congress Control Number: 2009922059

FSC
Mixed Sources
Product group from well-managed
forests and other controlled sources
Cert no. SGS-COC-003186
www.fsc.org
© 1996 Forest Stewardship Council

Print CO_2 compensated
Ident-No. 090576

Printed in Germany by Engelhardt und Bauer, an FSC-certified printer,
on FSC-certified Profisilk paper.

The book was printed at a plant which uses water power and solar
energy. A carbon-credit certificate was purchased for a total of 16.6
tons of CO_2 emissions.

BACK COVER Tree trunk in
the dense tropical forest
of Pohnpei, Micronesia.
Nourished by extraordinary
amounts of rain, this rugged
place teems with birds,
butterflies, lizards, and
hundreds of native plants
found nowhere else on Earth.